# FEAR

## FOR

# AMERICA

☆

## A TWITTER INITIATIVE

## OF THE

## U.S. DEPARTMENT OF FEAR

The Fear Press
Washington, DC

# DEDICATION

Chemical Industry

Correctional Services Industry

Defense and Homeland Security Industry

Entertainment Industry

Financial Industry

Food Industry

Health Insurance Industry

Oil Industry

Pharmaceutical Industry

Telecommunications Industry

*TIMENDI CAUSA EST NESCIRE*
Ignorance causes fear

— Seneca

# CONTENTS

# *FOREWARD*

## by the Secretary of Fear

Six months ago, with the Snowden leaks making headlines, CEOs of our corporate partners began calling my office, seeking reassurance. Could we weather this storm? I reminded them that although NSA was undergoing some difficulties, it was but one agency.

In these conversations I found myself looking for a document showing the full extent of our achievements during the Obama administration. However, because our operations are both multifaceted and highly compartmentalized—"alphabet soup" as they say—such a resource did not exist at the time.

When I consulted my staff, Undersecretary Wolf said she believed her social media team had the bird's eye view I was looking for. Wolf was right. Our "notorious" Twitter service (@FearDept) provided everything I needed. It is a repository of our accomplishments over a three-year period comprising our philosophy, values, and efforts to shape history-making events. I asked Undersecretary Wolf and her team to summarize our accomplishments in a report and include citizen feedback, hostile or not.

Our Twitter experiment is unconventional, but when I look at the Internet it is apparent we cannot afford to stand still. One concern we have is that "Twitter journalists" with no allegiance to the Department now act as news gatekeepers. They have taken the distribution of news out of the hands of our media partners and anointed sources that take an adversarial approach to our work. The Anonymous movement exemplifies this threat: some disseminate news, others make news.

Who are these social-media-empowered sources? What are their adversarial activities? Organizations such as the EFF (Electronic Frontier Foundation) and the ACLU (American Civil Liberties Union) relentlessly fire off FOIA (Freedom of Information Act) requests and sue us. WikiLeaks recently published over five million emails from Stratfor, a private intelligence contractor. Several U.S. publishers and at least two foreign broadcasting networks feature daily reports about our activities. Various authors have delved into our methods. We jailed Barrett Brown, but a handful of other investigative journalists still have jobs. Hundreds of bloggers, video-bloggers, webcasters, and podcasters regularly critique our programs.

Faced with a resistance movement online, the Twitter account serves our public relations agenda. The tweets have humanized our work, sometimes bringing to light the heroism of ordinary staff members. Whether it's an Occupy encampment on the night of our crackdown, or a tranquil village on the Indian subcontinent during a drone strike, there is nothing like hearing about it from the folks with their fingers on the buttons. We are also giving the public an inside look at the future of education, medicine, law, the arts, and the brew of chemicals that used to be called food. Tweet-by-tweet, as history-making events unfold, we tell our side of the story.

The Department's own managers and contractors will be studying this report. They need to see how we monitor anxiety levels in real time during National Fear Events. Experiments like #fearsharing and #1stAmendmentHours ought to serve as models for future cyber-democracy programs. Even when it's just a four-letter word, the feedback we get is useful. Let them think social media is all about them! Fear is what social media was created for.

In today's interconnected world, it's no longer enough that only our own citizens be frightened. Today some of the most innovative fear-making is happening north of the border and overseas. The report highlights the best practices of our foreign affiliates. We need to recognize their innovations and apply them.

We are humble shepherds working for wolves. My staff are proud of what we have achieved on behalf of our corporate partners—and justifiably so. I want to thank Undersecretary Wolf and her team at the Social Media Division for putting this report together. I want to express my profound gratitude to each of the 35,823 followers of @FearDept. This report affirms the importance of their tweets to the success of our mission.

Malcolm P. Stag III

Secretary of Fear
Washington, DC
January, 2014

# *PRAISE*

## for the Department

**@pbj06** The U.S. government has its own agency devoted to scaring you into submission and it's right here on Twitter

**@GlenAllenWalken** I think establishing a federal-level Department of Fear was a great idea.

**@0CommonSense** Thanks...you gotta be the most helpful federal agency ever! God Bless Big Government!

**@Kaveros** What the US Government would tweet if they were somehow forced to tweet the truth about everything.

**@timeoutcorner** Follow @FearDept to see what the US Federal Government is really thinking.

**@laurenalesia** Thank you for keeping us all informed about what horrors surround our Shining City on a Hill.

**@MarcosPedreiro** The US is cool because each month has a new threat! This month: Bioweapons. Thanks for telling me what to fear

**@poissonjensen** And they will keep on spewing fear until something sticks with the public... Distraction 101...

**@BeauregardB** To see how America is maintaining an adequate level of fear in its citizens... this is a "must follow" IMO

**@MeeMeeAlAradi** your statements are more accurate than @StateDept on almost EVERYTHING!!

**@MindDetonat0r** The Cult of "National Security" is the state religion of the United States. @FearDept is our temple, @SecFear our priest.

**@BringAhmedHome** #FF @FearDept though you've buried me alive, and I often wish I was dead.

**@Asshurtsmacfags** I seriously love and fear you at the same time. Is that weird?

**@RepublicanDalek** THE DEPT OF FEAR DOES EXCELLENT WORK, AND YOU SHOULD CELEBRATE THEIR EFFORTS TO THE EXTENT THAT THE SOUL-CRUSHING TERROR ALLOWS

**@MoenHj** Very well done job today. Keep people in the dark about NDAA while making them fear stupid shit. Way to control your minions.

**@AnarchistPrince** Why can't those people read actual news?! Your dept is too good at what it does.

**@charbouli** If you wanna hear the truth, follow the @FearDept

**@plumbermaz** With the GOP debates gone, @feardept has done a great job of filling up that void

**@PollyanaPinup** For a little wtf & adrenaline in the morning try @FearDept part of a complete breakfast **#truth #scary**

**@ma_dobberstein** Fear Dept. wants what's best for you. Even if that's a Hellfire missile through your window.

**@C0d3Fr0sty** Since the @FearDept is already watching you.. You might as well follow them. **#FF** @FearDept

**@bulldozia** There is nothing to fear but @FearDept itself.

# INTRODUCTION

A Twitter account (@FearDept) is operated as a public service by the Department of Fear (DoF). The objective of this account is "to promote the agency's agenda and increase public awareness of DoF and its mission."

The Department does basic research and development with the hope that it can be useful to its media or defense partners. In accordance with this mandate, we present *Fear for America: A Twitter Initiative of the Department of Fear.*

This report provides an overview of our activities and is divided into four sections: Part I looks at our colonization of social institutions; Part II examines how we are using laws, the courts and police to make the fear revolution permanent; Part III explores our wars and activities abroad; and Part IV looks at how we are dealing with the blowback, in other words, dissent.

Introductory paragraphs and titles from newspapers or videos are printed in italics. Comments by readers are in a smaller typeface than that used for tweets from the Department.

# PART I

# Building the Fear Society

# 1

# THE DEPARTMENT

**About the Department • About the Staff • Values • Jobs**

Without knowing what they ought to fear, US citizens might otherwise fail to support profitable national security initiatives. — SecFear

*The United States Department of Fear was established by an Executive Order signed by the Vice President in January 2004. The mandate of the agency is to promote fear in the interest of national security.*

## About the Department

In the race to the bottom, we're on top.

We call our vision post-partisanship. We see politicians helping corporations devise profitable solutions to America's problems.

**@iDiplomacy** Where's the Department of Hope?
After the election we talked him out of it.

## About the Staff

4.2 million of us have security clearances. **#TheOther1%**

Staff laugh when politicians threaten to cut our pay because we can always quit & make real money billing taxpayers as private contractors.

We won't hesitate to fire any staff member who exposes waste or corruption.

## Values

Security at any price.

Might makes right.

Justice is when the interests of our corporate partners prevail.

## Jobs

If you know any morally diminutive boot-licking climbers, please let us know. We'll have leadership positions open for them next year.

Students often ask about careers at Fear Dept. Because they need to pass a security clearance we say "never do anything fun or interesting."

# 2

# YOU THE PEOPLE

**Citizenship • Freedom • Activism • Patriotism • The Rest of the World • Personal Development**

You have to wonder about the true motives of people who attack the very policies that frightened Americans find most reassuring. — SecFear

*The focus of this chapter is human citizens, but over the years U.S. courts have extended the rights of human beings to corporations. In 1888 the Supreme Court ruled that corporations are people under the Fourteenth Amendment. In 2010 the court affirmed that corporations have the First Amendment right to make political donations.*

## Citizenship

From each citizen according to his or her lack of influence, to each corporation according to its need.

We're authorized to know things. The public isn't.

Some of you need to get off your high horse. Just because you're U.S. citizens doesn't mean we can't abuse you.

There are two kinds of citizens: those who support the activities of the Department, and those who know too much.

All citizens are equal but citizens with security clearances are more equal than others.

We're blessed with a population that believes in the Department's good intentions, and however much we shake them down, continues to believe.

Be thankful you're an American as we treat foreigners a lot worse.

## Freedom

Freedom is corporations making the big decisions for you.

It's a free country. If you don't want to get arrested, protest at home.

If you oppose our interests effectively, you'll find people start referring to you as a terrorist.

When citizens organize, we mobilize.

## Activism

What marijuana is to crack cocaine, social activism is to terrorism.

If you want to do activism, you've got to find a corporate sponsor. Otherwise the media won't take you seriously.

"They had it coming." Use this phrase when discussing protesters, whistle-blowers, journalists, or anyone we've assassinated lately.

In New York City, the difference between reckless drivers and protesters is we arrest protesters.

Warning: If you discover a legal and effective form of activism, we'll imprison you for terrorism.
**@_cypherpunks_** Come on, that's so unfair.

## Patriotism

Patriotism is knowing who to fear.

Do your best to live a lifestyle that's worth them hating us for.

The American Dream is landing a job with an intelligence contractor.

## The Rest of the World

Since the threat of total nuclear annihilation subsided with the end of the Cold War, the world has become a dangerous place.

Only 54% of Americans believe we're the top military power in the world. One third fear we're too weak.

## Personal Development

Have the heart of a CIA interrogator and the integrity of an FBI informant. Be drone pilot brave.

Do you cling to the fears we have given you, or do you make the effort to share them with others?

May we suggest you learn to behave as if everything you do is being recorded.

Just because you're paranoid doesn't mean we aren't after you.

Are you watching enough television? Eating enough processed foods? Remembering to drive when you could walk?

Don't just pull fears out of thin air. Watch television. Learn what scares the talk show hosts.

If you see where our corporate partners are causing a big problem then you should go fix yourself. See a professional, medicate, or read a self-help book.

We'll support just about ANYTHING that discourages critical thinking. That includes harebrained conspiracy theories that implicate the Dept.

# 3

# EDUCATION

**Principles • Good Parenting • K–12 • Higher Education • Discipline**

The more we squander on education the less we have to invest in drone warfare. — SecFear

*Education reform is as American as nuclear weapons. Efforts at reform go back to colonial times, yet progress has been slow— until the past decade. The new system rewards teachers who teach to the test and punishes teachers who don't turn their students into good test-takers. These and other changes have won the applause of the electronics and education industries.*

## Principles

If too many people enjoy learning something, we'll turn it into a subject of formal education.

The purpose of education is to turn inquisitive young minds into rule-followers.

If U.S. schools don't prepare American children for careers in the surveillance industry, all our spying will be done from India.

Our research shows people with high FQ (Fear Quotient) are more likely to support profitable national security policies.

## Good Parenting

Families that watch television together share more fears than families that don't.

*Homeless D.C. Families, Who Turn to the City for Help, Risk Triggering a Child Welfare Investigation*
Homeless with kids? Ask us for help and we'll take them away.

If your kids exhibit high energy, initiative or curiosity, get a doctor to prescribe them something.

Teach your kids to be conventional. If they stick out too much we're going to pound them down.

For young Americans, Security Clearance will be the ticket to a career. Responsible parents pick their children's playmates carefully.

## K–12

Support our War on Critical Thinking.

The United States Department of Fear is a proud partner of the For-Profit Education Industry.

We reformed education so students don't need to ask questions, only answer them.

Why did we introduce standardized testing in 2001? We noticed that countries with uncreative and obedient citizens had one thing in common.

## Higher Education

*Another Look at WikiLeaks (Or not?)*
Students and profs at our elite universities are too scared to read WikiLeaks documents.

We're pleased to report that federal and state spending on higher education is at a record low.

Choosing between college and prison? Not only are prison classes free, prisoners don't accumulate new debts to pay off.

**@joethecommunist** I got my phd from Folsom State Prison

*Colleges' Debt Falls on Students After Construction Binges*
Our bankrupt universities are driving students into debt to pay for luxurious facilities the students didn't ask for.

## Discipline

*Texas Honor Student Jailed for Missing Too Much School*
Honors student supports two siblings & works full time, but she missed class, so we're jailing her.

*Students Protesting Tuition Hikes Pepper-Sprayed by Police in Santa Monica, CA*
The students were protesting a 400% rise in tuition so we pepper-sprayed them.

*Extra Sleep May Improve Kids' Conduct.*
Perhaps, but drugging them is still more convenient.

Having the same companies serve both institutions streamlines the school-to-prison transition.

# 4

# PRISON AND OUR WAR ON DRUGS

**We're Number One • Achievements • Prisoners at Any Price • The Prison Experience • Medical Marijuana • Fighting Legalization • Profitability • Public Service Announcements**

At the rate we're locking people away, within decades non-prisoners will be the minority. — SecFear

*Mental illness afflicts half the population of the United States at some point during their lives. Although mental health services are not widely available, anyone caught self-medicating risks being locked up.*

## We're Number One

@hewritesthings According to a Human Rights Watch report, "the US continued to have the world's largest incarcerated population at 2.3 million." @FearDept Good work, boys.

*Growth Rate for Prison Exceeds That for Population Growth*
We lock people up at twice the population growth rate.

*What We're Doing About Louisiana's Prison Crisis*
The great state of Louisiana boasts the highest rate of incarceration in the world.

## Achievements

We turned the legal system into a profitable incarceration system. As long as people remain afraid, it will stay that way.

*Out of Prison, Into a Vicious Circle of Debt*
Rest assured we're doing everything we can to condemn lawbreakers to a never-ending cycle of despair.

*On Eve of MLK, the Mass Incarceration of Black America*
Mass incarceration has allowed us to roll back many achievements of the civil rights movement.

## Prisoners at Any Price

*Prison Industries: "Don't Let Society Improve or We Lose Business"*
@JohnRalphio I see you've created a business incentive to dissuade society's improvement. Nice.

*Plantations, Prisons and Profits*
Stiff sentences and lack of rehabilitation are the keys keeping Louisiana's privately run prisons profitable.

California state revenue allocations
Higher education: 10% (1980), 8% (2010)
Prisons: 3% (1980), 11% (2010)

*War on Drugs is a Trillion-Dollar Failure*
It's not whether you succeed, it's how hard you try.

*Man Behind Bars 2 Years After Judge Orders Release*
Our prosecutors are working to ensure innocent prisoners serve full sentences.

*Decriminalize Drug Use, Say Experts After Six-Year Study*
Then how are we supposed to fill our prisons?

*Unguarded Guardians: The Rampant Abuses of Our Prison Profiteers*
With leading corporations dependent on free U.S. prison labor how to maintain supply? Should debtors go to jail?

*Netherlands to Close Prisons for Lack of Criminals*
What happens when the drug laws are too sensible.

## The Prison Experience

*Forgotten US Inmate Drank Urine to Stay Alive*
The California student we jailed for five days without water hadn't been charged with any crime.

## Medical Marijuana

*Feds Raid Princeton of Pot in California*
We raided a medical marijuana university today.

*Houston Native Leads Quest to Legalize Pot in Calif.*
Richard Lee found pain relief in marijuana & is helping others live normal lives, so we're trying to destroy his life.

*Scientists Find Cannabis Compound Stops Metastasis In Aggressive Cancers.*
How to discredit this research?

## Fighting Legalization

*Record-High 50% of Americans Favor Legalizing Marijuana Use.*
Polls don't matter to us.

## Profitability

Votes to legalize marijuana in two states caused Corrections Corporation of America (NYSE: CXW) stock to drop 3.7%.

*The Shocking Ways the Corporate Prison Industry Games the System*
By incarcerating large numbers of immigrants, we restored the profitability of our private prison industry.

## Public Service Announcements

*Innocence Is No Defense*
The fact that you're innocent does not mean we can't imprison you for life.

We will fight the drug war to the last doobie.

# 5

# ECONOMY I – BONUSES FOR BANKERS

**Warning • The Classes • Our Corporate Partners • Banks • Labor • Walmart • Entrepreneurship • Personal Finance • Homes • Taxes • Defense Industry**

> Our system of government is one of "checks and balances": we cash taxpayers' checks and use the money to increase corporate balances. — SecFear

*Managing money and creating services to finance debt are the engines of our economy. Today the financial sector accounts for 8.4% of GDP and over 30% of corporate profits.*

## The Classes

The three main classes of our classless society: 1) persons with security clearances; 2) other investors; 3) persons under surveillance.

*DC Suburbs Now Contain 7 of the 10 Richest Counties in America*
We hire a lot of contractors.

It's unfair that the bottom 40% had to bear the brunt of the financial crisis. Next time the other 59% will have to share the pain.

*1.4 Million Families Live on $2 a Day Per Person*
Destitution is every citizen's worst fear.

Poor people can be profitable. The trick is to get enough of them together and figure out a scheme to take what little they have.

**Our Corporate Partners**

If you're one of our corporate partners, you want the taxpayers to cover your costs, not just your losses during a bailout.

Our corporate partners have the know-how to minimize public services and maximize shareholder value.

Rather than trickling down, our corporate partners' profits flood offshore investment opportunities.

The people may not always agree with everything we do, but they know we always have corporate America's best interests at heart.

In the market for suicide-inducing antidepressants? Tomahawk missiles? Toxic antibacterial soap? GMO seeds? High fructose corn syrup?

**Banks**

One Nation Under Wall Street.

In Derivatives We Trust

Stars = the 50 great banks of the 1980s. Stripes = the 14 great banks after mergers of 1990s.
@anon711 Except there are only 13 stripes.
We speak of the "14 great banks" as a sign of respect to a fallen bank. Washington Mutual, one of the 14, collapsed in 2008.

*How a Big US Bank Laundered Billions from Mexico's Murderous Drug Gangs*
The four pillars of our banking system are drug-money laundering, sanctions busting, tax evasion and arms trafficking.

Our friends at HSBC money laundered $800 million for the Mexican drug cartels, effectively bankrolling 99,667 murders.

The consequences of prosecuting HSBC execs for money laundering would be bad for investors, so we won't go there.

As expected @TheJusticeDept says "no viable basis" to prosecute @GoldmanSachs, our most trusted financial partner.

*Letter Carriers Consider Bringing Back Banking Services*
Beware the public option in banking.

## Labor

We're helping large businesses outsource good American jobs.

*The 40-Hour Work Week*
If we didn't make them work long hours they'd have time for politics and community groups.

To save humans for drudgery, we're building robots to do all the interesting jobs.

## Walmart

1.4 million Americans work at Walmart, making it the second largest employer in the U.S., just behind the federal government.

We believe in an America where every Walmart employee is paid enough to afford a car to sleep in.

*No Way Up: Walmart's Workers Decry Dead-End Poverty*
"Most of our employees have been at our store a great many years, mostly older women who are fearful." — Walmart worker.

## Entrepreneurship

Send your ideas for wars, weapons designs, and terror plots directly to corporations positioned to profit from them.

Where else can anyone who dreams up a new technology for killing, surveillance or data mining become a multimillionaire?

## Personal Finance

Yes, we're coming for your social security.

The more property you have, the less likely we are to take it all away from you.

*Debtor's Prison Legal in More Than One-Third of States*
Reminder: In many states we can send you to jail for not paying a debt.

*New Bankruptcy Law May Make It Harder for Hospitalized to Erase Their Debts*
We used to let people who get really sick keep some of their property, but now we take it all away.

Remember: Those of you who play by our rules and buy lottery tickets stand a chance of winning some of it back.

## Homes

*Whistleblower Gets Sham Justice from Wall Street Court*
Wall Street kindly offered to run a mandatory arbitration process for fleeced homeowners. Works as intended.

*Banks Shortchanging Consumers in Mortgage Settlement*
The banks deceived you, broke the law, took away your house, and threw your family on the street? Here's $2,000.

We're making it easier for people to rent back the houses they used to own before the banks wrecked the economy and got the houses.

## Taxes

Ever notice how in the name of going after a handful of untouchables, we only ever succeed at putting the screws on everybody else?

If you don't think of the taxes you pay to defend Mid East oil reserves as an oil industry subsidy or hidden fuel tax, that's fine with us.

We're always trying to come up with new ways to nickel and dime poor people. Since their numbers are growing, the small change adds up.

Our financial partners have never faced a problem too large for our taxpayers.

Pay the banks' debts or else.

**Defense Industry**

A fear shared is a share that trades higher (especially defense stocks). Use the hashtag **#MyWorstFear** to support the Department's work.

We figure as long as we are good at destroying things in Afghanistan, we don't need to build anything here (except prisons).

Countries don't need the weapons we sell them, but the U.S. economy—what's left of our manufacturing base—is dependent on this trade.

Inspired by Apple's announcement today that unlocked iPhones will be priced at $649, US House panel approves $649 bn in defense spending.

Three unlocked iPhones for every American at retail price. That's our defense budget for 2011.

Any system this expensive to defend must be precious.

**@AnonSikko** Can we haz peace?

We don't like the revenue model.

# 6

# ECONOMY II – AUSTERITY FOR PEOPLE

**Key Points • Austerity–USA • Austerity–Europe • Greece • Spain • Iceland**

> Our challenge is to convince people to sacrifice more, work harder, and be grateful for whatever the banks let them keep. — SecFear

*Austerity doctrine recognizes that if people are poor, it's their fault. To teach them a lesson, resources they could use to better themselves are transferred to financial institutions. The so-called PIGS of Europe (Portugal, Ireland, Greece, and Spain) are experiments in austerity. The United Kingdom is another.*

## Key Points

We like to tell other countries how to run their economies.

Freedom is countries opening their markets and financial systems to our corporate partners. Freedom is non-negotiable.

Our corporate partners dream of a world in which foreigners will be milked as easily as Americans.

## Austerity – USA

We'll be asking Americans to continue making personal sacrifices for the financial sector next year. Please do your part.

The reason we're asking younger generations to make larger sacrifices is pragmatic: they aren't likely to miss what they never experienced.

## Austerity – Europe

We view Europe's crisis as an opportunity to discredit everything European countries do better than us.

Where our banks make a wasteland we call it failed socialism in need of fiscal consolidation.

*How Greece Squandered Its Freedom*
After our financial partners rape a country, they have the New York Times publish a self-hating screed by a local.

## Greece

Democracy was born in Greece and we'd be happy to see it end there.

*How Goldman Sachs Helped Mask Greece's Debt*
Our pals at Goldman cut a lucrative deal with Greece that hid the country's debt.

Having lent the Greeks more than they could hope to repay, the banks have seized the opportunity to turn Greece into a debt slavery state.

*Greek Parliament Approves Austerity Bill*
Warned the nation was approaching "Ground Zero," the parliament of Greece has voted to impose severe austerity.

The Greeks remain too cowered to seize control of their destiny. Hooray!

@KeiaJin You have done your job well. i dunno why they think the banks have their best interests at heart.

Shut up and bend over Greece, Merkel is coming.

## Spain

We can't let the Spanish people win this one. They have to learn to take it like Greeks.

@elquedicemiau @FearDept Not gonna happen this time, pals. Sorry. We're kinda tired of being turned into pawns for everyone else's convenience.

When 100,000 march on the streets of Spain our media partners look for other stuff to report.

We've been watching live videos from Spain. It occurs to us those people don't tolerate as much abuse from their fear department.

## Iceland

Dogarnit! There's one country where our fear-mongering hasn't produced the intended results.

*Iceland Forgives Mortgage Debt for the Population.*
Shame! Shame!

We would sleep better if Iceland had not recovered to the extent it has. Iceland's recovery isn't something we care to hear discussed.

**#IcelandRecovery** is an inconvenient truth. What could make this model of economic recovery go away for us?

**#IcelandRecovery** isn't something we care to have widely understood.

**#IcelandRecovery** is not something we want people in Greece, Italy, Spain, Ireland, or Portugal to understand.

@**Beigemonster** I know your busy with internal matters, but when are you going to invade iceland? They are setting a bad example.

# 7

## OUR MEDIA PARTNERS

**Rules for Journalists • Some Headlines We Like • Arrests, Beatings and Intimidation • Citizen Journalism • Purpose of the Press • Methods of the Press • Mainstream Media • War • Foreign News • Cooperation • Propaganda • Hush**

> And our media partners, God bless them, wouldn't dare characterize a scientific law as "fact" if it seemed to contradict a statement by us. — SecFear

*In at least one respect, the U.S. media industry resembles the banking industry. Over the years small companies have merged to form larger ones. Today the "big six"—Walt Disney (ABC television) News Corporation (FOX News), Time Warner (CNN), Viacom, CBS and Comcast—control 90% of the media.*

### Rules for Journalists

Write what we say, ignore what we do.

As an American journalist, your first duty is to scare the public. Do that and you can break any rule in the book.

Journalists: Don't report facts at the expense of balance!

## Some Headlines We Like

*The Iranian Threat to New York City*

*No Letup Predicted in Terror Threat*

*Summer Holiday Could Tempt Terrorists, Federal Officials Warn*

*What Could Syria Do With WMDs?*

*Terrorists Seek Out "Friends" on Facebook*

## Arrests, Beatings and Intimidation

*Propaganda Contractor Admits to Running Smear Campaign
Against USA Today Reporters*
One of our propaganda contractors has admitted to running a
smear campaign against USA Today reporters.

*Dozens of Kurdish Journalists Face Terrorism Charges in Turkey*
100+ journalists languish in jail in Turkey. More than in Iran or
China. Twice as many as we arrested at OWS (Occupy Wall
Street) camps.

Correction to previous tweet. We've actually arrested more than 90
journalists for the crime of covering OWS protests.

In a country with a courageous press, our behavior toward
reporters would be a national outrage by now.

## Citizen Journalism

Reminder: Only select mainstream media journalists carrying
official Fear Dept. press passes may report OWS events.

LOL! The New York Times asks only that we not beat up NYPD
credentialed journalists. What about the others?

*So Then the FBI Sent Out an Agent to Check Up on My FOIA
Request*
**@DustinSlaughter** I'm thrilled that @FearDept now pays visits to no-good
citizens who file FOIA (Freedom of Information Act) requests. Fuck gov't
transparency

*Google Joins Copyright Police Force*
If our media partners accuse you, Google will demote you.

## Purpose of the Press

Is the news industry doing an adequate job of keeping citizens in the dark about what we're up to?

With the help of our media partners, we're confident that today's civil liberties nightmares will be welcomed as prudent security tomorrow.

Our news media partners help Americans connect with their fear of Iran.

Managed by a few trusted hands, journalism doesn't challenge our priorities or help people make informed choices about the big things.

The declining output and quality of professional journalism has proven a boon to the Department and the fortunes of our partners.

At election time, it's the responsibility of the media to ensure debate revolves around whatever cultural issues divide the 99 percent.

## Methods of the Press

Our news media partners know to focus on specific events of a democratic nature, not the big beautiful oligarchic picture.

U.S. journalists seldom insist we back up our rhetoric with evidence. That's not what our news media partners pay them to do.

The task of the American news media is to compare two parties' interpretations of our agenda.

## Mainstream Media

### *Fox News*

To pick up a new infection, it helps to spend some time in a hospital. Likewise, to pick up fresh fears, it helps to watch Fox News.

*It's Official: Watching Fox Makes You Stupider*
New study finds Fox News viewers know even less about politics and current events than people who watch no news at all.

## CNN

*CNN's Bogus Drone-Deaths Graphic*
Our media partner claimed we killed zero innocents this year.

*Why the World Is Ignoring Congo War*
Why? That's between us and CNN.

## MSNBC

*Rachel Maddow Fails to Question Guest Who Served as Top Pentagon Lawyer Under Obama About Drones*
Seeing we're in the midst of a killing frenzy, Maddow decided not to ask us about drones.

## The New York Times

We only have to hint what's fit to print.

We're pleased with the NYT. They published their story on the risks of domestic surveillance drones only AFTER Congress had approved them.

*What the New York Times Missed in Its 1st Article on Manning's Torture Hearing*
Our court martial of Bradley Manning is historic, but (thankfully) the NYT's coverage of the trial isn't worthy of a school newspaper.

## The Wall Street Journal

*Networks Ignore Reports That White House Shooter May Have Spent Time at Occupy D.C.*
Some of you predicted we'd blame "White House shooting" on **#OccupyDC**. WSJ has agreed to lead that smear campaign.

## War

Before and after we start a war, we count on our media partners to keep the public on our side. That's the purpose of American journalism.

It's our media partners' job to scare Americans about Iran. This way, we don't appear too pushy and the war comes as a relief to everyone.

Once we've scared them sleepless, we'll deploy the tried & proven therapy: Cable news coverage of our rockets firing over the Persian Gulf.

## Foreign News

*The White House Loves Aggressive Journalism—Abroad*
We believe the proper place for aggressive journalism is overseas.

*Why Is President Obama Keeping a Journalist in Prison in Yemen?*
A journalist was investigating our attacks too thoroughly, so we asked **#Yemen** to lock him up.

Today is World Press Freedom Day. Ever since WikiLeaks embarrassed us, we stopped protecting press freedom here. Our focus is defending press freedom abroad.

## Cooperation

In our kind of democracy the media ensure our activities do not become election issues.

*Hacking Book: How "Serious" Media Consigned WikiLeaks Cables to the Shadows*
Our news industry partners cooperated with us by hiding many shocking WikiLeaks revelations.

The banks rape entire countries behind their backs, but our media watch for protester misbehavior like hawks.

Our media understand that it is only by consistently repeating what we tell them that their reports come to have a truth-like quality.

## Propaganda

Facts are for wimps.

Bombing Libya killed no civilians (NATO S.G.), neither have drone strikes (J. Bremmer). And we arrested no reporters at OWS (NYPD Chief).

So what if we arrest our own journalists and lie about it? So what if we kill foreign civilians and lie about it? What's the big deal?

Pressing question: Since MSN isn't reaching young people, does the upside (low engagement) outweigh the downside (low propaganda exposure)?

The Department and our corporate partners think outside the left-right political paradigm. That box is for television viewing audiences.

*Opposition to Torture Decreases When the Word "Torture" Isn't Used*
So our media partners don't call it that.

## Hush

If it wasn't a major story in the media, we don't need you to know it.

CNN anchor shut up a Sikh man who tried to explain that the first American killed after 9/11 was a Sikh.

*Palestinian Prisoner Khader Adnan Ends 66-Day Hunger Strike*
Our media partners get it: Heroic non-violent resistance to arbitrary detention isn't something the public needs to know about.

# 8

## DEMOCRACY

**Campaigns and Elections • Voting • Our Parties • The Presidency • President Barack Obama • Congress • Our Corporate Partners**

America was founded on the ideal that profitable wars (War on Drugs, War on Terrorism, etc.) should trump the principle of self-government. — SecFear

*The United States has the lowest election participation rate of any industrial country.*

### Campaigns and Elections

In our kind of democracy campaign promises don't mean anything.

To increase your sense of security, which of your remaining freedoms would you like to see our presidential candidates debate taking away?

In a country where everyone perceives themselves to be above average at everything, declaring war on the bottom 47% is just good politics.

During the election candidates will again squabble about funding this or that bridge, bike path, or museum. If only the public knew where the money we get goes!

Think of your campaign donation as life insurance. No generous campaign donor has EVER been assassinated by an American president.

## Voting

Elections are the Supreme Court deciding the winner for you.

*Disgraceful: 6-Hour Lines for Early Voting in FL*
To prevent democracy from getting out of hand, we make Florida voters stand in line for up to 6 hours.

*Voter Fraud: Texas AG Threatens Election 2012 International Observers*
To help secure the elections, we're warning international observers not to enter polling places.

We let the citizens have their day.

## Our Parties

Name one of our activities that doesn't have bipartisan support.

By pushing the GOP rightward, we move the political center to the right. This way we control a party so lame it considers "center" a value.

## The Presidency

*Does The President Answer To The CIA?*
The president answers to us and not the other way round.

Staff debating whether Presidents' personalities guide our choice of weapon: cruise missiles (Clinton), jet fighters (Bush), drones (Obama).

We generally prefer Presidential candidates who have no record of military service because such leaders tend to be the more bellicose.

For the same reason it's easier for a Republican president to make peace, it's easier for a Democratic president to kill.

## President Barack Obama

The President has issued fewer pardons than his predecessor (Obama: 1, Bush: 11).

Polls show that this President has legitimated and increased public support for Fear Dept. policies.

This White House has made more of our activities more palatable to more Americans than any previous administration bar none.

## Congress

*House Deciding Whether to Fund Military or Social Programs*
No-brainer.

*Members of Congress Trade Stocks of Companies They Oversee*
Our congressmen know whether corporate lobbying efforts will succeed, so they make good stock traders.

## Our Corporate Partners

Don't mind where your money goes. Corporations sponsor politicians to do that.

The U.S. Dept. of Fear is vast but the quasi-private sector supporting our mission is several times bigger.

*Stealth Bill Aims To Cripple New Consumer Agency*
If our corporate partners can't control a key agency, they write a law that subordinates it to another.

These are exciting times. The corporate imagination has expanded to confront a citizenry holding rights they lack the resources to defend.

# 9

## POLITICAL EVENTS

**GOP Primary Debates • State of the Union Address •
Republican National Convention • Presidential Debates •
Presidential Election**

In America there is a place for politics. It's called
television. — SecFear

*Broadcasters know that almost $3 billion in advertising revenue is
up for grabs during a presidential election. As a public service, the
networks sponsor political spectacles featuring competitive fear-
mongering.*

### GOP Primary Debates

Which GOP candidate can be trusted to keep Americans
frightened? Staff will be live-tweeting the **#CNNdebate** on Wed.
evening from 8PM EST.

Santorum: "We are going to have a cataclysmic situation with the
most prolific [disseminator] of terrorism on earth."

Gingrich: "All of us are more at risk today than at any time in the
history of this country. This is a very sober period."

Romney: "The threat that doesn't get enough attention is
Hezbollah in Latin America." **#FearHezbollahLatinAmerica**

**@BennyBip** Who is scared?

**@MandeWilkes** I'm almost scared the baby in my belly is a boy, what with all these declarations of war on the stage tonight.

Let us kill them with our drones and we won't come for your little boy.

**@QsbfBreakfast** SERIOUSLY?! We're supposed to be scared of Cuba now?

Romney: "Iran could let off dirty bombs in the United States."

**@fbihop** We are on to the "Bomb Iran" part of the FLdebate.

**@starbeer** Wait -- did Santorum just say Iran is working with Fidel?

**@MattWilliams06** Again, Santorum refers to all of Iran as "the Jihadists."

Ron Paul would cancel our drug war. **#FearRonPaul**

**@Dowd_Timmerman** Is the entire Republican party other than Ron Paul afraid of the boogeyman? I've never heard so much scared talk in my life.

CNN debate summary:
**#FearHaqqaniNetwork** (Bachmann)
**#FearHezbollah** (Romney)
**#FearMilitantSocialists** (Santorum)
**#FearTerrorists** (Cain)

**State of the Union Address (SOTU)**

In debates GOP candidates presented our fear agenda. In the SOTU the president must convince Americans he should be the one to serve it.

No. of times the President uttered word "war" or "warfare" = 5; No. of times the President uttered word "peace" or "peaceful" = 1.

The real challenge of any SOTU is to convince the 99% to sacrifice more & be grateful for whatever the 1% allows them to keep (if anything).

**Republican National Convention (RNC)**

*Iran Turns the Screws on Dissidents Ahead of Elections*
We'll do it in August at the RNC in Tampa.

*CNN Compares Protesters to Terrorist Insurgents*
To garner public support, we're demonizing protesters prior to the conventions.

Abusing protesters is one aspect of a convention. Inside hotel rooms politicians try to convince donors they can sell profitable fears.

Mitt Romney's address tonight has been designated a National Fear Event of the United States Department of Fear.

## Presidential Debates

*Police Arrest US Presidential Candidate Jill Stein at Debate Site*
In preparation for tonight's debate we arrested the Green Party's presidential candidate.

## Presidential Election

Our 2012 election pits the party with the strongest record on assassination against the party with the strongest record on torture.

In Nov. we'll let you choose between a President who knows how to assassinate Americans and a former governor who knows how to fire them.

We're asking you to choose between false hope and no hope.

*Fact Check: President Obama Has Aggressively Pursued and Addressed National Security Leaks*
Obama campaign touts the fact his admin prosecuted a record number of whistle-blowers under the Espionage Act.

The President seems to believe the key to his re-election is proving he has internalized the core values of the Department. We're flattered.

# 10

# THE ENVIRONMENT

**Earth Day • This Land is Our Land • Environmentalists • Natural Disasters • Hurricane Sandy • Fracking • National Parks**

If we cut down all the forests and fished out the sea, think how much money we could put in the bank for future generations. — SecFear

*The United States is the world's number one consumer of oil and number two burner of coal. The Pentagon is the top polluting organization in the world, producing more hazardous waste than the five largest U.S. chemical companies.*

## Earth Day

Imagine if all the other countries did for the earth what we've done for the earth.

We say there can never be enough dams, parking lots, and big box stores.

It's our earth.

## This Land is Our Land

*Sioux Tribes Upset Over Sale of Sacred Site in SD*
To make sacred Sioux land appealing to strip mall developers, we poured tax money into a road.

We're always looking for new ways to stick it to the American Indian. It's hard though because in the past we were extremely thorough.

## Environmentalists

*As Eco-Terrorism Wanes, Governments Still Target Activist Groups Seen as Threat*
Our broad definition of domestic terrorism gives us an excuse to spy on many environmental activists.

## Natural Disasters

We're not sure it was smart to warn the public about **#Irene**. If a hurricane disappoints, media & govt lose credibility making our job harder.

*Obama Officials Pushed to Underestimate Gulf Oil Spill*
When oil spilled into the Gulf of Mexico we asked our scientists for estimates but ended up using our own.

Our response to the BP oil spill was to expand offshore oil drilling; our response to Fukushima was to build nuclear reactors.

*Fukushima: Mark 1 Nuclear Reactor Design Caused GE Scientist To Quit In Protest*
Say "BP oil spill" and everyone knows what you mean, but not if you say "GE nuclear meltdown" (i.e. Fukushima).

Our media partners ensure environmental disasters don't get named after American companies (BP Oil Spill = OK; GE Nuclear Meltdown = Not OK).

*Shell Arctic Ocean Drilling Stands to Open New Oil Frontier*
Bored with polluting the Gulf of Mexico, our oil industry partners asked if they could drill in the Arctic Ocean.

## Hurricane Sandy

Protecting our partners in the financial industry remains our first priority.

Our top priority has been securing Goldman Sachs H.Q. (now behind sandbags).

Friendly reminder: Stay inside. If you start wandering the streets looking desperate or hungry, you're fair game for our mercenaries.

Any looting by hungry citizens or attempts by the homeless to find shelter should be reported to us immediately.

## Fracking

Tap water on fire? Try bottled water.

Flammable tap water is a small price to pay for a boom that enriched our friends at Goldman Sachs.

*New Proposal on Fracking Gives Ground to Industry*
Lobbyists convinced us drillers shouldn't have to disclose their chemicals to landowners until it's too late

Going camping this summer? Be sure to introduce the family to fracking water. It tastes best mixed with artificially flavored drink mixes.

China's rapid progress towards full toxicity is enviable, but when it comes to fracking, they're three years behind.

## National Parks

*House GOP Bill Could Devastate National Parks*
In the name of improving border security, we are preparing to devastate our National Parks.

We plan to waive all environmental laws within 100 miles of our N and S borders, destroying 25% of the national parks.

# 11

## FOOD

Agricultural Subsidies • Seeds and Pesticides • GMO and
Monsanto • Nutrition • Antibiotics • The Future of Food

Quite frankly, we would rather risk the health of 100
million people than put a $100 million dent in corporate
profits. — SecFear

*From 1994–2012 subsidies for corn, a raw material for most
processed food, totaled $84.4 billion. In 2009 the U.S. spent over
$15 billion in subsidies for corn, cotton, rice, wheat, and soybeans,
but only $800 million on subsidies for vegetables and organics.*

### Agricultural Subsidies

The United States Department of Fear is a proud partner of the
Processed Food Industry.

As we enter a period of self-imposed financial hardship, demand
Congress increase subsidies for US agribusinesses.

To keep junk food affordable, our 2008 Farm Bill provided billions
in direct payment subsidies to corn and soybean growers.

*Dispute Over Labeling of Genetically Modified Food*
We won't let Americans decide for themselves how safe U.S.
grown food is.

*Why Supermarket Tomatoes Tend to Taste Bland*
Ever wonder how we learned to grow the world's most tasteless vegetables?

*Report: World Changes Eating Habits as Food Prices Soar*
Fear Diet going global? High food prices spell big opportunity for American producers of low-cost processed foods.

## Seeds and Pesticides

The United States Department of Fear is a proud partner of the Seed and Pesticide Industry.

Ten companies control 89% of the global agrochemical market.

Brand name seeds account for 82% of the commercial seed market worldwide. With our help, Monsanto & DuPont dominate.

*Dow Corn, Resistant to a Weed Killer, Runs Into Opposition*
We intend to approve DowChemical's application to market a derivative of Agent Orange for use on corn crops.

@poissonjensen The same DowChemical's who hired Stratfor to spy on Bhopal victims and activists...

*Chemical Exposure Influences Rat Behavior for Generations*
Rats exposed to a common fruit and vegetable fungicide display increased ANXIETY for three generations.

## GMO (Genetically Modified Organism) and Monsanto

In GMO We Trust.

Having discussed the matter with Monsanto, we decided Americans don't need to know what's in their food.

*WikiLeaks: US Ambassador Planned "Retaliation" Against France over Ban on Monsanto GMO Corn*
We threatened EU countries with retaliation if they banned GMO foods.

Support our policy of not labeling U.S. food. Trust us, you don't really want to know what's in it.

*2012 California Propositions: Monsanto: 9 Contributions,
Totaling $8,112,867*
Californians voted not to label GMO foods. Our corporate partners
got the results they paid for.

We're looking at replacing indigenous fish and animal species with
patented GMO varieties.

French scientists fed Monsanto GMO to 200 French rats.
Accustomed to tourte parmerienne, of course they all died.

## Nutrition

It's a free country. If you don't want to eat poison, grow your own
food.
@iamn0one but you outlawed growing our own food

*Open Letter to the U.S. Government About the Quality of Food Aid*
Letter we received from Doctors Without Borders urges us to stop
supplying nutritionally substandard food to malnourished children.

*Remarks on Global Food Security*
While admitting our diet isn't all that nutritious, Secretary Clinton
urged the world to embrace our food industry partners.

*High School Students Protest Healthy Lunches*
Our kind of protest. We don't call them "Generation Fear" for
nothing.

## Antibiotics

*Antibiotics Victory Will Preserve Medicines for Sick People, Not
Healthy Livestock*
A federal court had ordered us to take action against farms that
feed antibiotics to livestock.

*U.S. Seeks Voluntary Antibiotic Limits in Livestock*
We invite those of our corporate partners who care to do so to
voluntarily limit the use of antibiotics in livestock.

*Health Chief Warns: Age of Safe Medicine Is Ending*
The World Health Organization says to stop using antibiotics in
food production. Hmm we'll ask the food industry what to do.

We are committed to ensuring factory farms have access to the antibiotics necessary to maximize the profitability of the fast food industry.

## The Future of Food

*Who Will Control the Green Economy?*
The "Green Economy" holds the promise of a convergence and concentration of corporate power.

# 12

## HEALTH

**Drugs • Toxifying • Vaccines • Revenue Model • Health Tips • Trends**

Even our most intractable political problems have pharmacological solutions. — SecFear

*The United States spends 18% of GDP on health care—one third more than any other major developed country. U.S. businesses spend nine times more on employee health care than foreign businesses.*

### Drugs

The United States Department of Fear is a proud partner of the American Pharmaceutical Industry.

@**moche8** Big Ag makes you sick so Big Pharma can sell you drugs! The system works fine.

*"Prozac Defence" Stands in Manitoba Teen's Murder Case*
Judge found Prozac caused boy to commit murder. Given who their advertisers are, our media partners don't report this.

*More ADHD Drugs, Fewer Antibiotics for U.S. Kids: Study*
Since 2002 prescriptions of **#ADHD** medication to American children have increased 46%.

## Toxifying

The United States Department of Fear is a proud partner of the Chemical Industry.

We'll spend billions to defend you against a speculative terrorist threat, but won't warn you if there's a pesticide (triclosan) in your soap.

*FDA Rejects Call to Ban BPA from Food Packaging*
We've decided BPA is good for you.

*Chemical Companies, Big Tobacco and the Toxic Products in Your Home*
Our babies are born with the world's highest levels of flame retardants in their bodies. **#Number1inFireproofBabies**

*Tribune Watchdog: Playing with Fire*
We made sure the furniture in your home contains toxic fire retardant chemicals that do nothing to prevent fires.

4.9 billion pounds of flame retardants are sold yearly in the U.S. The chemicals save no lives, but they're linked to cancer, anxiety...

The purpose of our FDA is to give consumers some false assurance: profitable chemical X hasn't been banned, so it must be safe.

## Vaccines

After meeting with drug company CEOs, we determined American babies need twice as many shots as other countries' babies.

## Revenue Model

The United States Department of Fear is a proud partner of the Health Insurance Industry.

Our partners include the world's most profitable hospitals.

We're showing the world how to make the management of medicine more profitable than its practice.

*Hospital Chain Inquiry Cited Unnecessary Cardiac Work*
Our medical partners convince healthy people to undergo lucrative open heart surgery.

## Health Tips

Turn off the television once a week and go shopping.

We recommend a diet rich in soybean and corn products with chemical additives for color and flavor.

## Trends

Although 33 nations have lower infant mortality and 37 have longer life expectancy, our healthcare system is the world's most profitable.

*List of Countries by Life Expectancy*
In the Americas only Cubans, Chileans, Cost Ricans, and Canadians live longer than Americans.

*Last year, 36% of Americans Ages 19–29 Couldn't Afford Needed Medical Care, So They Went Without*
All soldiers get medical care.

*As Young Lose Interest in Cars, G.M. Turns to MTV for Help*
Nation in Crisis Update: Unpatriotic young Americans opting for bicycles and public transit over automobiles and debt.

When industry is to blame for a crisis, our media partners are responsible for diverting public anger from politics into lifestyle tweaks.

# 13

## CULTURE

**Arts • Music • Poetry • Film • Dance • Photography • Awards • Thanksgiving • Other Holidays • Literacy • Olympics • Exploration • Space Program**

Building up words and images is more profitable than building up people. — SecFear

*Culture has consistently ranked among the largest U.S. exports. In 2011 the motion picture industry supported 2 million American jobs and generated $104 billion in wages.*

### Arts

*Teacher Survey Shows Morale Is at a Low Point*
One in three U.S. teachers said their schools lost arts, music and foreign language programs. #FearArt

*The Pepper Spraying Cop Meme*
Arts Calendar. The Lt. John Pike Collection at GMOM (Gallery of Memorable Occupy Macings) has opened to the public.

### Poetry

Whatever happens
we have got
the Predator Drone,
and they have not.

## Music

♫ We see you when you're sleeping
We know when you're awake
We know if you've been bad or good
So be good for goodness sake! ♫

**@pfhawkins** Huh I always thought it was "so conform for goodness sake!"

**@AhmadoofGlory** ♪ Get your drones running Head out on the skyway Looking for militants. And whatever comes our way.♪

## Film

*Zero Dark Thirty Revealed: Five Things You Need to Know*
For her film "Zero Dark Thirty" about our raid on OBL, we fed Bigelow a story we hope will redeem our torture program.

## Dance

**@TJDanceParty** Meet us at the jefferson memorial 4p on the 4th of july. Lets celebrate our indepenDANCE from the policestate!

Terrorism.

**@raine1967** on July 4th I plan to dance with my husband at the Jefferson Memorial. **#nothingcanstopme**

We'll see about this.

Dance on Ayatollah or Mao's shrine and you get arrested. Jefferson was a greater man than both, making the crime worse.

## Photography

If you have a hobby, try to pursue conventional projects. Creativity may raise neighbors' suspicions and lead to unnecessary reporting.

*Chronicles of a Paranoid Nation: The Deciduous-Infrastructure Factor*
We caught David Hobby (@strobist) photographing critical deciduous infrastructure.

*Joint Regional Terrorism Center: Terrorism Indicators & Warnings*
"Videotaping, photographing or sketching of buildings not of interest to visitors or tourists should be reported."

*Illinois Partnership Targets Agro-Terrorism*
AgroTerrorism Indicator. "Unauthorized photography of processes at facilities in or around farms."

*Police Say They Can Detain Photographers If Their Photographs Have "No Apparent Esthetic Value"*
Summer Travel Tip: Tourists should only photograph things "a regular tourist would photograph."

## Awards

This time of year the buzz around the water coolers is how many Department staff will be nominated for the Nobel Peace Prize.

## Thanksgiving

*Bottom 80 Percent: 7% of Financial Wealth*
Be thankful for your slice of the pie (it will be smaller next year).

*Black Thursday*
Happy Thanksgiving! We commend Walmart for forcing many of its employees to spend the holiday serving customers.

We are thankful that more people don't stand up to us.

We are thankful for our two parties.

We are thankful for the pathetic governments of Europe.

**@Casual_Obs** I'm thankful for @feardept

**@Anon_Central** We are thankful for activists and journalists for remaining ignorant to @FearDept's tweets. Truth shall be hidden as always.

We're thankful for our 5,113 nuclear warheads.
**@SickDos** the 13 coincidental?!?
Supposed to be 5,115 but 2 are missing.

We're thankful for our prisons and the companies that run them for us.

**@JohnnyArgent** More prisoners per capita than ANYBODY! We're NUMBER ONE!!! USA! USA! USA!
Prison to the people! Cheers!

Thankful we are to those who spread the Department's message. You keep staff morale high even on days we can't find protesters to beat up.

## Other Holidays

Flag Day is celebrated on June 14. Contact us if you have reason to believe that one of your neighbors is not participating.

**@JSDwyer** Approaching St Patricks Day I'm reminded British gov/police treated Irish much like US gov/police increasingly treats Americans.

## Literacy

Ever since we started torturing people leading news media have acknowledged that words mean what we say they do.

The destruction of thought begins with the corruption of language.

For example, use the word "socialism" as a synonym for "bad." If you don't like something, just call it socialist.

The word "genocidal" means any regime we're scheming to overthrow: Iran, Syria etc.

*French Bookstores Still Prospering*
What to do about France?

## Olympics

*London's Dystopian Olympics: Criminal Sanctions for Violating the Exclusivity of Sponsors' Brands*
The city with the best plan for a police state gets to host the Olympics.

Our corporate partners will be competing for mindshare in London for the next two weeks. Join us in supporting their quest.

## Exploration

*Is There Life on Mars? NASA Curiosity MSL Will Find Out*
If we find life should we license, enslave or kill it?

If we find water on Mars, it could be a lot more cost effective to send terror suspects there than to prisons on the moon.

Tonight's landing on Mars was certainly entertaining. Nevertheless, it hardly compares to the night we told you we got bin Laden, does it?

Curiosity. What an unfortunate name. That's something we've been trying to stamp out with standardized testing.

**@RepublicanDalek** LOOK AT IT THIS WAY: YOU'VE EXILED CURIOSITY TO MARS

**Space Program**

*Seeing Red: Anger as NASA Announces Plans to Cut Funding for Missions to Mars*
Realizing drones should explore our own citizens' backyards first, we're cutting Mars exploration.

It's great to be ending the era of U.S. space exploration on a high note. We plan to integrate NASA with defense & sell the civilian parts.

As for space exploration, maybe China will be interested in continuing where we left off.

# PART II

# Leading the Fear Revolution

# 14

## THE WAR ON TERROR

**We're Winning • Strategy • Threats We're Watching • Survey
• Alerts • Fearsharing • Terrorism Research • Our Targets •
Lists • NEW! Nigerian Terrorists • Somali-American Check-
Writing Terrorists • Material Support • Recruiting Muslim
American Patsies • Entrapping Young American Muslims •
Muslim American Internet Terrorists • Beyond Muslim
Americans • Cyberthreats**

We've humiliated the terrorists by demonstrating that our
capacity for self-destruction is vastly greater than anything
they can inflict. — SecFear

*The War on Terror has cost an estimated $4 trillion or $16,000 per
citizen. The most conservative death toll is 225,000. The profits of
our five largest defense contractors have increased 450% since
2002.*

### We're Winning

We've got Americans scared shitless of just about anything
attached to the word "terrorism." Even if it's just a chunk of
software code.

*As a Target for Terrorists U.S. Ranks Number 41 in World*
For terrorism overall, we're number one.

The financial crisis and Hurricane Katrina—such self-inflicted catastrophes have made the terrorists feel impotent. So yes we're winning.

*Obama Moves to Make the War on Terror Permanent*
Bless him!

## Strategy

The threat of al-Qaeda gives meaning to the sacrifice of liberty.

*Was Saudi Arabia Involved?*
We're 100% committed to pursuing any terrorist who doesn't appear to have high-level connections in Saudi Arabia.

*Bin Laden May be Dead but Bin Ladenism is Still Alive.*
Ladenism. Fear it. **#FearLadenism**

If we didn't have terrorists to fight over there, how would we position ourselves to keep the world's oil reserves in friendly hands?

Real terrorists have gone low tech so as to fly under our radar. Alas, much of our costly surveillance tech is useless for monitoring them.

Long-term, you can't beat humint (human intelligence) for results. But Washington has a drone lobby, a missile lobby. There is no humint lobby.

## Threats We're Watching

Although terrorist attacks have declined considerably, we've inflated the threat to fantastic proportions!

*Documents Reveal al Qaeda's Plans for Seizing Cruise Ships, Carnage in Europe*
Our colleagues discovered plans for terror attacks encoded on the porn video the terrorist had hidden in his underwear.

*"Inspire" al-Qaeda's English-Language Magazine Returns Without Editor Awlaki*
Oh no it's back.

*Official with Knowledge of Threat Says It's "Specific Enough to Elicit Worry"*
Worry.

*FBI's Terrorism Search Goes Undersea*
After this comes space, the final frontier.

## Survey

What terror group are you most afraid of these days?
**#fearsharing**

**@TerribleAuthor** DHS for me. Oh and Public Schools.

**@MindDetonat0r** The corporate mafia in DC.

**@AyeshaKazmi** Quite funny that all answer ive seen so far are related to the US govt.

## Alerts

We encourage Americans to retweet terror alerts.

## Fearsharing

Your followers are probably curious how the recent terror alert makes you feel. Help us realize the power of social media.
**#shareyourfears**

Don't selfishly cling to the fears we have given you, make an effort to share them with others. That's why we gave you social media.

**@suzannelemaa** ...scared out of my mind about what terrorists are going to do to us for killing bin laden.

**@fullmetalmarty** Looks like the @FearDept is winning with all this Bomb stuff.

**@LukeG95** I was going to go to London this weekend. But I got scared that we would be bombed by terrorists.

**@Tori_Terhaar** Up late ..saw on the news about someone trying to bomb a airplane or something.. have to fly on the 18th scared

**@biTRACIal** On a train that stopped for 10mins at 42nd street due to police activity. I got nervous

**@Camdenjoseph** this "failed" car bomb... was actually a successful terrorism attack. it freaked people out

**@JakePlunkett** Times Square. More like Times Scared. Am I right? **#dontbescared**

**@Army_chic86** We have a new Terrorist Leader and yet America is worried about this Weiner guy & his pics.

Sad but true.

## Terrorism Research

*Research Funded by Homeland Security Discovers Manhattan Most Targeted U.S. City*
Who would have thought?

*Radical U.S. Muslims Little Threat, Study Says*
We wish the researchers good luck with their next grant application.

## Our Targets

Is America too dependent on foreign enemies? Can increased exploration for domestic threats fill the gap?

Today we regard almost every American citizen as a potential terrorist.

If we accuse you of being a terrorist, then you are guilty of being a terrorist.

Your web-browsing habits are a sure give away. At least that's what we'll tell the jury. **#terrorism**

Keep filling out those credit card applications. In the event of another attack we will be sending you shopping. **#patriotism**

If we charge you with terrorism, you had better plead guilty. Defense attorneys know the outcome if a prosecutor says "al-Qaeda" to a jury.

If we're being brutally honest with you, it's only because after so many years of being lied to, most of you can't take it.

First we came for the American Muslims. Nobody gave a shit. Then we came for the anarchists...

## Lists

*Baby, 18 Months Old, Ordered Off the Plane at Fort Lauderdale Airport*
Their 18 month-old was on our no-fly list, so we humiliated the parents.

*Mandela Dropped from U.S. Terrorism Watch List*
We removed the 1993 Nobel Peace Prize winner from our terrorist watch list four years ago.

*US No-Fly List of Terror Suspect Doubles in 1 Year*
Our no-fly list doubled last year from 10,000 to 21,000 (including 500 Americans). **#progress**

The closer we get to defeating al-Qaeda, the more names we add to the no-fly list.

**@stacyherbert** Oh great, I see that the U.S. Dept. of Fear – @FearDept – has just added me to Watch List Number 1.

**@stacyherbert** @GonzaloLiraSPG I am not at liberty to respond to that tweet as @FearDept is now monitoring my tweets.

## NEW! Nigerian Terrorists

*Exclusive: U.S. to Slap "Terrorist" Label on Nigerian Militants.*
NEW TERRORIST GROUP DECLARED

Labeling Nigeria's "Boko Haram" a terror group gives us an excuse to spy on the Nigerian community & arrest old people who reply to the emails.

## Somali-American Check-Writing Terrorists

*Found Guilty of Raising Money for Somali Terrorists*
Great how "material support" broadens definition of terrorism!

We can think of no better use for your tax dollars than protecting Somalia by keeping a Somali-American check-writer in jail for 15 years.

*Somali Islamists Offer 10 Camels as Bounty for Obama*
Oh dear.

*Found Guilty of Raising Money for Somali Terrorists*
Up on "terrorism" charges? Trial outcome is forgone conclusion.
@nkocurek There are trials?!
@nkocurek Still going to have nightmares about terrorists lawyering up.

## Material Support

Every citizen has reason to fear he or she may be providing material support for the terrorists—without knowing it.

*Former Miami Cab Driver Grateful That Feds Dropped Terrorism Charges*
We dropped the "material support for terrorism" charges against the Miami taxi driver who's life we've been ruining.

*Ex-Michigan Rep. Gets One Year for Lobbying for Charity with Terrorism Ties*
We gave the other guy 5 years.

*Muslims Say NYPD Surveillance Is Already Changing Behavior*
If we charge any of these citizens with material support, they know they can't win. It makes surveillance frightening.

## Recruiting Muslim American Patsies

*Fake Terror Plots, Paid Informants: The Tactics of FBI "Entrapment"*
Should our fake terror plots target less vulnerable people?

We're looking for a few gullible men with dark complexions and well below average IQs.

Can't pass any of your classes? We're recruiting low achievers for special missions.
@Diplopundit Where have you been all my life? Sign me up!

## Entrapping Young American Muslims

*Teen Charged in Terrorism Plot*
We charged the 15 year old, but only questioned the 6-year-old.

*Judge: U.S. "Created" Synagogue Terror Plot*
Judge claims we seized upon a man's "fantasies of bravado and bigotry," and then made those fantasies come true.

Whereas the FBI invents bomb plots to entrap Muslim-Americans, it is the responsibility of the CIA to entrap Muslims living abroad.

**Muslim American Internet Terrorists**

*Three Men in NC Terror Ring Get 15–45 Years in Prison*
The words he wrote on Facebook were "disgusting," said the judge, referring to the crime for which Yagi got 32 years.

*A Dangerous Mind?*
Some things Mr. Mehanna wrote were in such bad taste that we're putting him in prison for 17.5 years. **#speechcrime**

*Saudi Student Convicted of Terrorism in Texas*
Jury has convicted a Saudi student on WMD terrorism charges on the basis of his blog & some Internet sites he visited.

**Beyond Muslim Americans**

*Kellyville Man Arrested for Terrorism*
Citizen, angry about noisy power line crossing his property, tried to take a pole down. We charged him with terrorism.

*Former Marine Held Involuntarily Over Facebook Posting*
Brandon Raub, a vet, called us "evil" on Facebook so we took him away.

*Five Men Arrested in Plot to Bomb Ohio Bridge*
We turned 5 anti-bank "anarchists" into Terrorists by supplying them with explosives.

*Anonymous Spokesman Barrett Brown Faces New Charges*
We're charging @BarrettBrownLOL with posting a link. Have you done this?

*DHS List: You Might Be a Domestic Terrorist If...*
List of political views that get you put on a "terrorist watch list" is far broader than we had previously indicated.

Schedule: This week we're coming for the **#anarchists**; Aug 7–13 **#WikiLeaks**; Aug 14–20 **#socialists**; Aug 21–27 **#anonymous**

Schedule (con't): Aug 27–Sept 3 **#environmentalists**; Sep 4–17 **#tradeunionists**.

## Cyberthreats

*More Americans Worried About Cybarmegeddon Than Terrorism*

*Twitter: The Terrorists' New Favorite Social Network?*
Twitter terrorism. Fear it.

"The U.S. is Facing an Attack Threat Equivalent to 9/11 ... a Cyber Pearl Harbor."

Music to our ears.

All they have to do is take out Facebook and every American would lose friends and family. **#NationalCyberattackFearMonth**

@d3Fn I will never understand how sitting at home in your underwear pressing buttons is terrorism or criminal.

# 15

# WAR ON TERROR EVENTS

## Preparations for the 10th Anniversary of 9-11 • 10th Anniversary Terror Threat Surfaces • We Planned a Scary Event for 11-9-11

The measure of the success of a National Fear Event (NFE) of the U.S. Department of Fear is the level of concern or panic the event creates. — SecFear

*The #fearsharing potential of social media is unprecedented. To make the most of threats, the Department tweets major fear events.*

## Preparations for the 10th Anniversary of 9-11

@jimhofmann Air raid sirens going off in DC. Other twitter types say its a problem at the National Cathedral.

@crunchychocobo Should I be disturbed by the sound of air raid sirens outside?

@brandonworley The air raid sirens here in Zanesville. Air raid sirens sounded in OH

## 10th Anniversary Terror Threat Surfaces

*U.S. Sees "Credible" 9/11 Terror Threat*
Yes we're acting on the terror threat. Having made a list of America's remaining freedoms we're deciding which to exchange for security.

**@lay_boo** Everyone, please stop tweeting about the terror threat. I'm scared and I'm going to cry.

Pay no attention to such requests.

**@katiiieex** scared shitless of this terror threat on new york...

Thanks for sharing.

**@IndianDerima** Literally started crying when i heard we have a terror threat in nyc

This tweet brought tears to our eyes.

**@GagaIsMyLifeBTW** Terror threat !!! Omg in NYC !!! & DC !!! @ladygaga be safe !!

**@Tishya_Khillare** Don't know whether to go to office tomorrow or not coz of the terror threat.

BREAKING: 9/11 anniversary passes without incident on the continental United States.

## We Planned a Scary Event for 11-9-11

*Emergency Alert System to be Tested*
We've planned something frightening to mark 11-9-11: Our first nationwide test of our Emergency Alert System (EAS).

Countdown: 13 Minutes! Today's test of the EAS has been designated a National Fear Event (NFE) by the United States Department of Fear.

Countdown: 10 Minutes! Staff is taking shelter. Please go to your nearest television. **#NationalFearEvent #EmergencyAlertSystem**

Countdown: 3 Minutes! You should now be seated in front of a television in a secure location. **#EAS #NFE**

Countdown: 10 Seconds.

**@timeoutcorner** Duck and cover, bitches.

Thank you for participating in a National Fear Event (NFE) of the U.S. Department of Fear.

**@timeoutcorner** Boy that was a lot of fun. Thanks.

# 16

## HOMELAND SECURITY

**SWAT • Militarizing Police • Local Police • New Name for DHS • Chalk Crime • Empire State Shooter • Mass Shootings • Walmart Shooting • Terrorism Hot Spots**

No town is too small or too remote to qualify for counterterrorism grants for SWAT training, surveillance gear. — SecFear

*The number of SWAT (Special Weapons and Tactics) raids had increased from only 3,000 in 1980 to more than 80,000 by 2011. Every day over 100 Americans have their homes raided by a SWAT team. Special grants have enabled local police departments to acquire counter-terrorism equipment tested on insurgents in Iraq and Afghanistan.*

### SWAT

*SWAT Team Fires Semi-Automatic Weapons at Unarmed Teenage Girl*
We fired semi-automatics at a teenage girl hiding in her room during a routine SWAT raid in Delaware.

*Grenade Burns Sleeping Girl as SWAT Team Raids Billings Home*
When we raided the wrong house in Montana we threw a flash grenade at a bed and a small girl got fried.

*Terrorized Family: SWAT Team Raids Wrong Home*
Don't confuse the girl we burned this week in Montana with the
one we traumatized last week in Delaware.

*Fully Armed SWAT Team Shoots Ex-marine 71 Times in
Marijuana Raid*
Our SWAT team shot ex-Marine Jose Guerena 71 times in an
Arizona marijuana raid.

*Vegas Police: Officer Fired 7 Shots into Vet's Car*
In Vegas Monday we killed an unarmed Gulf War vet with 15
rounds from an AR-15 rifle.

*Marine Killed by SWAT Causes Outrage in Arizona*
Don't confuse the unarmed vet we blew away in Vegas on Monday
with vet we blew away in Arizona in May.

## Militarizing Local Police

*Police Deploy Weaponized Drones to "Enhance Protection and
Safety of Citizens"*
As part of our efforts to militarize U.S. police, we sent Texas a
drone that can fire a taser.

*Sound Canons Used on Block Party*
This university town in rural Illinois seemed the ideal place to test
our new sonic weapon.

Just as many dead terror suspects never set eyes on a U.S. soldier,
tomorrow's incapacitated protesters won't see our police officers.

@jaykelly26 can anyone tell me why @FearDept has a truck with RPG guards
used for "Homeland Security"?

## Local Police

*German Police Fired Just 85 Bullets Total in 2011*
In 2011 we fired as many bullets at one unarmed person as were
fired by German police the whole year.

*Handcuffed Man Shot Twice by San Francisco Police – Witness
Reports*
It's easier and more convenient to shoot a suspect after we've got
him in handcuffs.

*Anaheim Police Fire Non-Lethal Rounds, Release Dog on Families*
Saturday we shot **#Anaheim** residents with rubber bullets and sicced our dog on them.

*Jonesboro Police Chief Defends Officers, Admits Claim Handcuffed Man Committed Suicide "Defies Logic"*
This report explains how Chavis Carter committed suicide while handcuffed in the back of our car.

Houses shot-up, women raped, child abducted, church looted... Just another night in ~~Kabul~~ Flint.

@JacobyNelson Please do not use Kabul in the same sentence as Flint. It makes Kabul look worse than it is.

LIVE SPEECH: Watch Sen. Lieberman scare people into funding costly new Homeland Security projects.

*Anti-Terrorism Data Sharing Puts American Freedoms at Risk*
Our fusion centers will spread misinformation about a citizen throughout the entire country.

In the event of a homeland security incident, would Canadian troops be reliable? Or should we go with a private contractor?

**Support our wars against #terrorism, #WikiLeaks, #Mexicans, #drugs, #Anonymous and #whistleblowers.**

**New Name for Homeland Security**

Should we rename homeland security? Your opinion counts.

@JamesFallows "Dept of Security Theater" #NewName4DHS

@kade_ellis BENDOVER is by far the best. Omg so good.

**Chalk Crime**

If you see someone drawing on a sidewalk, say something. **#chalkupy**

Chalk + sidewalk = chalkcrime.

*Mom Scheduled to Serve Community Service for Chalk Vandalism*
We apprehended a chalk terrorist in Virginia and sentenced her mother.

Ever wonder what we'll have you arrested for?

## Empire State Shooter

*U.S. Drone Strikes Kill 18 People in Pakistan*

*Eleven People Shot, Two Fatally, Outside Empire State Building*
We KILLED 18 people in Pakistan today. That's almost twice as many as the Empire State shooter SHOT.

Don't confuse guys with drones with guys with guns. One killing spree is not like another.

Firing guns at a man 8 feet away, we'll injure 9 innocents. Firing our missiles at a man 25,000 feet below, any witnesses don't survive.

## Mass Shootings

*168 Children Killed in Drone Strikes in Pakistan Since Start of Campaign*
"I saw men, women and children die during that time. I never thought I would kill that many people." — Drone Pilot

When we kill school children, it's always for a good cause.

## Walmart Shooting

*Black Friday Violence: Two Shot in Wal-Mart Parking Space Dispute*
Doesn't matter who was there first, the bigger SUV gets the parking space.

## Terrorism Hot Spots

*Study Lists San Diego County as Terrorism Hot Spot*

*Colorado Cities Make Terrorism "Hot Spot" List*

*Rural Hot Spots Point to Terrorism Threats*

*Study: Manhattan the Most Targeted Spot in U.S. by Terrorists*
Nevertheless, Every Good Town Deserves Security Pork

# 17

# TASERS AND OTHER TOYS

**Guidelines for Using Tasers • Tasering Facts • Tasered People
• Case Study • Health Risks • Future Technology**

Surveillance technology and robotics will make most police
officers redundant within a few years. But we won't tell
them that. — SecFear

*Taser International has sold 720,000 Taser weapons around the
world. Its customers include 16,000 law enforcement agencies. In
one third of 900 taserings investigated by the Houston Chronicle in
2007, no crime was being committed and no person was charged.*

## Guidelines for Using Tasers

If you don't follow our orders within 17 seconds, we're allowed to
taser you.

@NOH8ER can we haz tasers too? #selfdefence

## Tasering Facts

*Tasers Have Killed at Least 500 Americans*
We've killed at least 500 Americans over the last decade with our
tasers.

*Naked 80-Year-Old Woman "Raising Cane" Gets Tased, Arrested*
We use our tasers to discipline citizens, even great grandmothers.

*Police Shot Children as Young as 12 with 50,000-Volt Taser*
We use our tasers to discipline citizens, even 12 year-old girls

*Naked Houdini Shrugs Off Stun Gun*
We've yet to develop a taser that's effective against nudity

**Tasered People**

*Baby Shot with Taser*
We were not aiming the taser at the 2 year-old child.

*Police Taser Woman Cutting in Line at McDonalds Drive-Thru*
A Fayetteville woman jumped the line at a McDonald's drive-thru so we tasered her twice and pulled her from her car.

*Caught on Tape: Can't Speak English, Brutally Tasered by Police*
When a Chinese woman in New Hampshire tried to buy more than two iPhones we tasered her for Apple.

*Police Use Stun Gun On Pregnant Woman in Dispute Over Ticket*
A pregnant Chicago woman tore up her parking ticket so we tasered her.

*A Ticket, 3 Taser Jolts and, Perhaps, a Trip to the Supreme Court*
Chicago didn't pioneer the tasering of pregnant women over torn-up tickets. Seattle started it. **#creditwherecreditisdue**

*Cop Threatens Men for No Reason*
They were shooting a video outside a Walmart store so we scared them away with our tasers. **#Houston**

**Case Study: Testing our Tear gas in Egypt**

@sharifkouddous Tear gas fired right near makeshift hospital. Unbearable. Doctors patients forced to flee

@sharifkouddous People all very aware that this endless supply of tear gas is from US. "Made in USA"

In Egypt we're really famous for our tear gas. In other countries we're better known for our bombs.

@sharifkouddous Tear gas manufacturer is "Combined Tactical Systems" based in Pennsylvania.

Lots of speculation on Twitter about the ingredients in the gas security forces at Tahrir are using against protesters.

Listen Egypt, it's not mustard gas you're choking on until NPR says its mustard gas.

**Health Risks**

*Tasers Pose Risks to Heart, a Study Warns*
Tasers identify 340 defective hearts in 10 years.

*How Dangerous is Pepper Spray?*
During a 30 month period 26 people died because their lungs were found to be defective when we pepper sprayed them.

**Future Technology**

*Mind Reading and Brain Computer Interface Technology: The Future is Coming, Fast*
To keep America safe, we're developing mind-reading tech. and brain implants.

Our limo fleet up 73% since 2008: many "armored to protect against attack" or for "surveillance or undercover ops."

*Google Begins Testing Its Augmented-Reality Glasses*
Share your vision with us.

*Future Riot Shields Will Suffocate Protestors With Low Frequency Speakers*
New type of riot shield patented by Raytheon promises to hinder the ability of protesters to breathe.

# 18

## BORDER ENFORCEMENT

**Deportations • That American Girl We Deported • Borders •
Internal Checkpoints • Fences**

No other country is so tough on illegal immigration they
deport their own citizens. — SecFear

*According to the Pew Center, net migration between the U.S. and
Mexico in 2012 was zero. Nevertheless, that same year taxpayers
spent $11.7 billion on the security of the U.S.-Mexico border—the
most on record. The borders are the responsibility of Immigration
and Customs Enforcement (ICE), a division of Homeland Security.*

### Deportations

*Thousands of Kids Lost From Parents in U.S. Deportation System*
If a non-citizen mother reports domestic violence, we'll seize the
opportunity to deport her.

*Parents Deported, What Happens to US-Born Kids?*
To expedite the deportation process, we take kids away from
parents & put them in foster homes.

*Obama Administration Has More Prosecutions for Illegal Re-
Entry Than Any Other Crime*
Illegal re-entry accounts for nearly 50% of all federal criminal
prosecutions & carries sentences of years in a Corrections
Corporation prison.

## That American Girl We Deported

*Dallas Teen Missing Since 2010 was Mistakenly Deported*
Two years ago we accidentally deported a 14 year-old American girl to Bogota, Colombia. They now have her in jail.

The 14 year-old American girl we mistakenly deported to Colombia didn't speak Spanish at the time. But she does now.

We told the American girl we accidentally deported to Colombia she must pay for her own plane ticket home.

*U.S. Immigration and Customs Enforcement: Leadership*
Does deporting a 14 year old American citizen to Colombia warrant any resignations? Nah.

*Homeland Security (ICE) Deporting War Veterans Under New Laws*
We don't only deport 14 year old U.S. citizens, we also deport veterans.

## Borders

*Rock-Throwing Prompts Border Shooting, U.S. Says*
That rock-throwing kid we shot dead on the Mexican side? We're investigating the incident as "an assault on a federal officer."

*U.S. Testing Surveillance Balloons on Mexico Border*
We're putting equipment from Afghanistan and Iraq to use along our 100 mile-wide border.

You know what was even funnier? When we said we needed billions to secure our northern border from "the terrorists," they believed us!

We're making the world's borders invisible to our corporate partners. In return, they're helping us make borders impenetrable for people.

## Internal Checkpoints

@cjohanns Yikes! When you enter Maricopa County in Arizona, you know it! Just saw four cops in army fatigues and assault rifles.

Sounds like @cjohanns has encountered one of our internal border checkpoints.

## Fences

*For First Time Since Depression, More Mexicans Leave U.S. Than Enter*

Build that fence! They're escaping!

# 19

## TSA

**Incidents • Porno Scans and Pat-Downs • Philosophy • Policy**

Is there a line in the sand, a point beyond which we can push citizens no further? Is there no indignity the people will not meekly suffer? — SecFear

*In 2001 taxpayers paid $725 million to private companies to staff airports with low paid, poorly-trained, under-motivated screening personnel. In 2011 taxpayers gave $8.1 billion to the Transportation Security Administration (TSA) to buy scanning equipment and staff airports with low paid, poorly-trained, under-motivated government employees.*

### Incidents

*Woman Arrested at Austin International After Refusing Enhanced Pat Down*
Citizen wouldn't let us touch her breasts so we put her in handcuffs & dragged her across the floor.

*Family's Outrage as TSA Pats Down Their Daughter*
Meanwhile at JFK we terrified a 7 year-old mentally handicapped child with cerebral palsy.

*TSA Defends Pat-Down of 4-Year-Old at Kansas Airport*
In a statement, we defend our pat-down of a 4-year-old terror suspect at the Kansas airport.

## Porno Scans and Pat-Downs

*Rand Paul's Pat-Down Standoff With TSA in Nashville Ends*
We don't porno scan or grope passengers on private jets. Sen. Rand Paul should travel by corporate jet like the other senators.

*Priest Defrocked for Child Sex Abuse Now Works for TSA, Report Says*
We hired a defrocked Catholic priest to supervise your TSA pat-downs at Philadelphia International.

Actually, TSA screening is an experiment. We're trying to find out if there's a line we can't cross.

## Philosophy

*Passenger's Implant Claim Triggers Flight Diversion*
When a passenger claims she has "something implanted in her body" but doctors find no scars, we scramble our F-15s.

From our perspective, even speculative threats that defy the laws of biology and physics have terror scare-potential.

How likely is it explosives some dude put inside a Harry Potter book could blow up a bridge or that a woman with no scars is carrying a body bomb?

The public isn't capable of rationally assessing whether a particular terror scenario is physically possible or even remotely probable.

## Policy

*Report on Federal Air Marshal Service Paints an Unflattering Picture*
We treat our air marshals as if they were postal employees. What's the worst that can happen?

*TSA: Fail*
Despite all our intrusive behavior, luck remains the most important element in airport security.

# 20

# COURTS AND THE CONSTITUTION

### Our Courts • Supremacy Clause • Treason

If you don't like what we're doing, complain to one of our judges about it. — SecFear

*The number of Supreme Court cases won by members of the U.S. Chamber of Commerce rose from only 43% during the years 1968 to 1986 to 68% during the years 2006 to 2010. According to a study cited in the Wall Street Journal, 40% of federal verdicts favoring employees are reversed on appeal, while only 8% of pro-employer verdicts are reversed.*

## Our Courts

Our Supreme Court says Congress may re-copyright public domain works.
**@the_erased** Oh come on.

*Wal-Mart Wins. Workers Lose.*
Liberty! Our Supreme Court frees corporations & shareholders from risk of losing class action lawsuits.

*Supreme Court Sides With Wal-Mart In Sex Bias Case*
American women concerned about wage equality can enlist in the military. Nobody is forcing them to work at Walmart.

*Democratic Senators Issue Strong Warning About Use of the Patriot Act*
We have top-secret intelligence operations based on secret legal theories that aren't crucial to national security.

*U.S.: Dismiss Lawsuit Over Americans Killed by Drones*
When we were sued for assassinating that American boy we had our judge toss the case on a technicality.

**Supremacy Clause (Part 6, Section 2)**

*Article VI, Clause 2 of the Constitution is known as the Supremacy Clause. In addition to the Constitution and federal statutes the Supremacy Clause establishes U.S. treaties as "the supreme law of the land." The U.S. has signed and ratified various treaties prohibiting torture and requiring that officials who order torture be prosecuted criminally.*

~~Universal Declaration of Human Rights~~

~~International Covenant on Civil and Political Rights~~

~~Convention against Torture or Other Cruel, Inhuman or Degrading Treatment or Punishment~~

~~Geneva Conventions~~

*Appeals Court Says CIA Can Hide Torture Evidence from Public*
Our court has ruled torture is an "intelligence method" so it's noyfb.

*John Yoo, Former Justice Department Lawyer, Protected from Torture Lawsuit, Rules Appeals Court*
People we torture have no rights. Zero. Got that?

When we torture not the device but the interrogator gets credit but when we kill from the sky the technology gets all the credit.
**#unfair**

*State Department's Top Lawyer Stepping Down*
Harold Koh, the anti-torture advocate who we let serve as our top lawyer in exchange for his soul, will step down.

We're grateful the Obama White House and Justice Dept. worked overtime to cover-up our criminal activity during the Bush administration.

**Treason**

~~No Person shall be convicted of Treason unless on the Testimony of two Witnesses to the same overt Act or on Confession in open Court.~~

*Jose Padilla and How American Justice Functions*
We tortured Padilla for 5 years then showed a scared & patriotic jury a jihad camp application form with his name on it.

# 21

## THE BILL OF RIGHTS

**Context • 1st Amendment • Free Speech Zones • Free Speech Hours • 2nd Amendment • 4th Amendment • 5th Amendment • Gitmo**

Why carry people off to prison when you can bring prison to the people? That's the beauty of the Free Speech Cage.
— SecFear

*The 1st to 10th amendments of the Constitution are known as the Bill of Rights, ratified on December 15, 1791. Citizens of the new republic wanted to be sure they would not lose any freedoms they had enjoyed as British subjects. The individual freedoms enumerated by the Bill of Rights stem from the English Bill of Rights and the Magna Carta. The former provided an early precedent for the right to keep and bear arms and prohibited cruel and unusual punishment, whilst the latter inspired the right to petition and trial by jury.*

### Context

We advise politicians to exercise discretion, picking rights to champion only after consultation with lobbyists.

"The Constitution does not give us rights" — Rick Santorum

We couldn't have said it better.

## 1st Amendment

~~Congress shall make no law abridging the freedom of speech~~

The First Amendment is in effect when we say it is; during the times we specify; in places of our choosing. **#OccupyLA**

*Homeland Security's Domain Seizures Worries Congress*
A few Congressmen just woke up to the fact we go around seizing domain names for alleged copyright violations.

*What Counts as Abetting Terrorists?*
Reminder: Talking to or advocating on behalf of designated Terrorist groups is "materially supporting" them.

*Muslim Pleads Guilty to Using Internet to Solicit Murder and Encourage Violent Extremism*
Today we charged a man with "using ... the Internet to place others in fear." **#chutzpah**.

## Free Speech Zones

We invented the Free Speech Cage.

We believe every U.S. city should have a small fenced-off space where citizens can speak freely under police surveillance.

Free speech cages (aka 1st Amendment zones, free speech zones, & protest zones) are areas we set aside for free speech.

**@Jtitoj01** We can now form in small units and speak from a cage like animals.

**@anonoccubloc** Frees Speech Zone = Preliminary Detention
Aw, they're catching on.

## Free Speech Hours

First Amendment Hours are your designated time periods for free expression. We try to keep you posted as to the schedule.

Your **#1stAmendmentHours** this week: Wed. 13:00-16:30 ET

**@kevl9987** petitioning to extend **#1stAmendmentHours** by 2 hours

Your **#1stAmendmentHours** expire in thirty minutes. You should now be wrapping things up.

@jcerwinske Giving @FearDept a big "FUCK YOU" while there is still time!

Five minutes. It's time to delete whatever project you were working on.

## 2nd Amendment

The answer is surveillance. If we know when people are opening their gun cabinets we can get SWAT to their homes in time.

We discourage media speculation about whether shooter took antidepressants. However, it's OK to ask if marijuana or illegal drugs involved.

*List of Mass Shootings Worldwide and Associated Antidepressants*
For internal use only.

*Colorado Mass-Murder Linked to Prescription Drug Use*
Not important.

*Prozac-Like Drug Luvox was Being Taken by Teenager Responsible for Littleton Columbine High School*
Not important.

Both guns and games are dwarfed by pharmaceutical sales. If any industry has to take the bullet you know which one it won't be.

## 4th Amendment

~~The right of the people to be secure in their persons houses papers and effects against unreasonable searches and seizures shall not be violated~~
~~and no Warrants shall issue but upon probable cause~~
~~supported by Oath or affirmation & particularly~~
~~describing the place to be searched and the person or things to be seized.~~

The Fourth Amendment basically talks about privacy, and we're just not comfortable with that.

These days we'd much rather kill a suspect than take him to court.

The law says we have to get a warrant to spy on U.S. citizens. But we don't think we should ever be forced to prove we got a warrant.

*Supreme Court Upholds Jail Strip Searches, Even for Minor Offenses*
Hooray!

Please be advised your pre-plea punishments—tasering, pepper-spraying, gassing, & stick-beating—will now be followed by a strip-search.

## 5th Amendment

~~No person shall be deprived of life, liberty or property without due process of law~~

*How Extremism is Normalized*
If we put you on our hit list, your 5th Amendment due process rights will be satisfied by internal deliberations.

*Getting Away With Torture*
Our federal appeals court ruled that American citizens we torture should not be allowed to sue us.

## Gitmo (Guantanamo Bay Detention Camp)

As recently as June 2009 an overwhelming majority of Americans supported closing Guantanamo.

*Poll: Support For Closing Guantanamo Grows*
The President knows there's no political cost to stomping on the legal rights of Gitmo detainees.

*Poll Finds Broad Support for Obama's Counterterrorism Policies*
Support for Guantanamo detention is up to 70% from 40% in 3 yrs, meaning we've almost doubled the # of chickenshits.

Guantanamo Prison costs U.S. taxpayers $800,000 per year for each of our 171 inmates.

*The 40 Prisoners Still Held But Cleared for Release At Least Five Years Ago*
After clearing a Gitmo inmate for release, we like to hold him another 5 years.

*Military Limiting Guantanamo Detainee Access to Lawyers*
To make the President look tough, we're reducing Gitmo detainees' access to lawyers

Taking away Gitmo detainees' few legal rights is a no-brainer.

Obama could water-board detainees with his bare hands and not lose votes.

*American Sits Almost a Year With No Charges in Isolated Bolivian Prison*
How dare they!

# 22

# THE NEW LEGAL SYSTEM

The Four Freedoms • Rule of Law • When Public Opinion
Matters • Two-Tiered Justice System • Equal Justice for All •
Worldwide War • Patriot Act Renewal • Patriot Act 10th
Anniversary • KSM • Espionage Act • The More (Laws), the
Better • Conviction Rate • Criminalizing Protesting

If we actually tried to do what most citizens suppose to be
our job, it would be hard to make the case for so many of
the new laws. — SecFear

*On May 21, 2009 President Obama gave a speech at the National
Archives (aka "the tomb of the U.S. constitution"). The title of his
speech was "Protecting Our Security and Our Values." Observing
that the fear of terrorism had not diminished, the President
proposed changes to the U.S. legal system. The speech was music
to the ears of Fear Department staff. Here was a professor of
constitutional law declaring that the ancient law of the land would
no longer suffice: the terrorists are too scary for it.*

## The Four Freedoms

Every American has the right to help us lie our way into another
war.

LEADING THE FEAR REVOLUTION

Every American has the right to call for the assassination of people who expose our war crimes.

Every American has the right to advocate the preemptive use of WMD against countries that scare them.

Every American has the right to incite the Department to violence against its enemies.

## Rule of Law

*Some U.S. Drone Attacks May Be War Crimes*
President chooses his victims carefully, so can't be.

When the UN asks us to provide a "legal basis" for the drone assassinations we blow them off.

## When Public Opinion Matters

*Poll Finds Broad Support for Obama's Counterterrorism Policies*
A Feb. 2012 Washington Post-ABC News poll found 83% approve of our secretive drone assassination program.

It's not a war crime when public approval for the policy is above 80%.
**@Proofer3** The Hague SPECIFICALLY begs to differ
We don't report to no Hague ma'am.
**@angryneary** what's a Hague anyways? A fish?
We love our citizenry.

*More Americans support torture to fight terrorism, poll finds*
In fact, once public approval for water-boarding approached 50%, it was clear that torture did not constitute a war crime.

Until we've secured public support for a crime, we do everything we can to keep it "out of sight, out of mind."

96

## Two-Tiered Justice System

*Dept of Justice Mysteriously Quits Monsanto Anti-Trust Investigation*

*No "Viable Basis" to Prosecute Goldman, Justice Department Says*

*HSBC, Too Big to Jail, Is the New Poster Child for US Two-Tiered Justice System*
Among all developed nations, we boast the finest two-tiered justice system.

## Equal Justice for All (of the 99 Percent)

*Yes, America, We Have Executed an Innocent Man*
No one can ever say again with a straight face that we don't execute innocent men.

Better that ten men who were probably guilty of something anyway be executed than one guilty man go free.

**@KimDotcom** I have no fear because I have done nothing wrong!
He's not afraid right and wrong don't matter to us?

When citizens take us to court, we either win on technicalities or by claiming the evidence threatens national security.

## Worldwide War

*Congress Endorsing Military Detention, a New AUMF (Authorization for the Use of Military Force)*
S1867 is a declaration by Congress that the entire world is our battlefield and the war will never end.

## Patriot Act Renewal

USA PATRIOT Act (Uniting and Strengthening America by Providing Appropriate Tools Required to Intercept and Obstruct Terrorism Act).

*Democratic Senators Issue Strong Warning About Use of the Patriot Act*
Two US senators claim the public would be stunned to know what we think the Patriot Act allows us to get away with.

The PATRIOT Act was extended by 4 years in May 2011. Congressional support was overwhelming. People are scared.

When we demand info on a citizen the party who receives our demand is CRIMINALLY PROHIBITED from discussing our demand.

**Patriot Act 10th Anniversary – 2011**

10 years ago we didn't have the liberty to spy on law-abiding citizens or search them without a warrant.
**#HappyBirthdayPatriotAct**

@CuriousLemming yep! As a criminal defense atty I can vouch for that There's no Fourth Amendmnt anymore so we'd better hold on tight to the Second.

The PATRIOT Act gives us the liberty to sneak'n peak.

*A Tool in the Government's War on Privacy? Absolutely. But in Its War on Terror? Not So Much...*
Last year less than 1% of our Sneak'n Peak searches were terror-related. 76% (2,779) were drug-related. **#FearWeed**

@CuttingEdgeHist Sneak & Peak! –You never hear about this verse in Greenwood's "Proud to be an American"

**KSM (Khalid Shaikh Mohammed)**

*In a Reversal, Military Trials for 9/11 Cases*
Safety first. KSM too scary to put on trial in NYC to face military commission.

@PJCrowley prosecution of #KSM by military tribunals undercuts our global promotion of the rule of law.

The US legal system is 234 yrs old, but its time has passed. Khalid Shaikh Mohammed inspires Obama to design a new system. Change at last!

**Espionage Act of 1917**

*Daniel Ellsberg: "Obama Would Have Sought a Life Sentence in My Case"*
In the past 3 years we've charged twice as many under the Espionage Act as in the previous 95 years.

## The More (Laws), the Better

*Private Purchasing of Prisons Locks in Occupancy Rates*
Want fewer dumb laws? Sorry, our agreement with the prison industry stipulates 90% occupancy for 20 years.

Our laws make sense when considered from the perspective of those they were written for.

*The Many Failed Efforts to Count Nation's Federal Criminal Laws*
Do you really want to cross us? We have more federal criminal laws at our disposal than anyone can count.

## Conviction Rate

*The Myth of Our Weak Justice System*
Between 2000 and 2005, 99% of the 435,000 federal criminal defendants we prosecuted nationwide were convicted.

## Criminalizing Protesting (HR347)

*HR 347 "Trespass Bill" Criminalizes Protest*
House passed a law prohibiting protests in the vicinity of the President or Secret Service agents.

@d_seaman Congrats on your new law making peaceful protest illegal. A real home run!

@kade_ellis what did you do to keep the media so quiet about HR347

@LordDunalley "(1) a fine under this title or imprisonment for not more than 10 years.." WTF?

@LordDunalley Are you trying to make protesting a felony?!

@digitallofi How do we ensure 90% occupancy for prisons for the next 20 yrs? Get @FearDept to declare protesting an act of sedition...

# 23

## NDAA 2012

**Debate and Passage • NDAA Countdown • Presidential Waiver • They Take Us to Court**

Tonight NDAA became the law of the land. I want to thank Congress, the President, and especially our news media for making it happen. — SecFear

*The National Defense Authorization Act of 2012 (NDAA) included a provision for the indefinite detention of U.S. citizens without trial. Although it involved a serious point of U.S. law and became the subject of a lively and colorful congressional debate, most mainstream media organizations gave it little coverage.*

### Debate and Passage

Under our new new legal system terrorism suspects will be held in "prolonged detention" inside the U.S. without trial.

Staff are monitoring live video of U.S. senators plotting the indefinite detention of Americans on our behalf.

*The Media's Blackout of NDAA is Shameful*
We're grateful for it.

NDAA permits the indefinite detention without trial of "citizens" which is understood by us to mean anyone without real money or political power.

## NDAA Countdown

~~nor be deprived of life, liberty or property without due process of law~~

~~Fifth Amendment to the United States Constitution~~

NDAA Countdown: 3 Hours!

**@inspac3** well shit.

**@GirlWithHat13** @FearDept God help us.

**@nail_gun** doomsday has arrived

NDAA Countdown: 2 Hours!

**@CulturalHistor** @FearDept I wonder how many of us will have our front door busted open in the morning.

NDAA Countdown: 1 Hour 30 Minutes!

**@CLeg5** Is Guantanamo ready to handle the influx of all these Americans?

**@twopartsnet** Nice knowing you US democracy. You too, liberty.

~~In all criminal prosecutions the accused shall enjoy the right to a speedy and public trial~~

~~Sixth Amendment to the United States Constitution~~

~~to be informed of the nature and cause of the accusation~~
~~to be confronted with the witness against him~~
~~to have compulsory process for obtaining witnesses in his favor~~
~~and to have the Assistance of Counsel for his defence.~~

NDAA Countdown: 1 Hour!

Shut Up. You Don't Get a Lawyer.

**@RachunZero** Have you started an "office pool" for the first journalist held under NDAA? Is Assange already taken?

NDAA Countdown: 45 Minutes!

**@GhostIsMyHost** Why did no one see this coming?

NDAA Countdown: 30 Minutes!

~~Magna carta cum statutis angliae~~

**@losarot** @FearDept Hey FearDept, Is my FEMA camp bed ready and waiting, I think I should be heading there pretty soon.

**@deezthugs** Hmm... Google "privacy policy" and NDAA go into effect at the same time

## NDAA Countdown: 20 Minutes!

**@Some_1_dy** what does this mean tell me i heard about the sweep and im over here setting up traps. i have a family what do you mean by this?

**@GirlWithHat13** Watched it. NDAA is the worst betrayal I've ever known.

## NDAA Countdown: 7 Minutes!

**@oldschooldsl** RIP - The United States of America - July 4, 1776 – March 1, 2012

**@PimpthugAi** what's this countdown for!

## NDAA Countdown: 5 Minutes!

As mentioned, there's a major party going on here. Staff and lobbyists are now gathering around the podium for the final countdown.

## NDAA Countdown: 3 Minutes!

## NDAA Countdown: 1 Minute!

**@FatTonyCologino** I'm going to spend my last two minutes running outside naked.

**@conrad108123** It has been nice while it lasted hasn't it?

**@ishtarmuz** So who is going to burn down the Capital Building? Isn't that next? **#1932**

## NDAA Countdown: 0 Seconds!

Staff are cheering!

Oh my... They're chanting now: Detain them! Detain them! Detain them!

**@FurPawsRadio** Grab your guns folks, were fucked. @FearDept and **#UnitedStatesIsNotTheLandOFTheFree**

**@Roy_Talks** We're All Fucked

New chant: "Arrest them! Arrest them! Arrest them!" It could be the alcohol. Staff have abandoned any pretense of civility.

**@CLeg5** @FearDept So what are we allowed to say, now that we don't have rights?

ATTENTION CITIZENS / TERROR SUSPECTS: The National Defense Authorization Act for Fiscal Year 2012 (NDAA) is now in effect.

Statement issued by @SecFear thanks the Washington political establishment for the NDAA, singles out the news media for special praise.

## Presidential Waiver
*How President Obama Plans to Implement the NDAA's Military Custody Provisions*
Whereas yesterday your liberty was secured by law, today it is secured by presidential waiver.

## They Take Us to Court
**@JSDwyer** Told about #**NDAA** my mom asked incredulously "why aren't they talking about this on the NEWS?"

*U.S. Anti-Terrorism Law Curbs Free Speech and Activist Work, Court Told*

*Federal Court Enjoins NDAA*
Chris Hedges' lawsuit undermines the "broad, menacing detention powers" NDAA gives us.

BREAKING: A federal judge temporarily blocked NDAA provisions that allow indefinite detention of Americans.

*The House (Further) Militarizes U.S. Detention Policy*
In the name of fixing NDAA, the House is considering amendments that entrench & expand military detention.

*Co-Counsel Speaks After NDAA Hearing*
Our power to detain U.S. citizens perpetually, even if they aren't members of a terrorist group.

*U.S. Judge's Rule Protects Reporters, Activists in Their Middle East*

BREAKING: Slapping us in the face, Judge issues permanent injunction against "indefinite detention" provision of NDAA.

**@iwelsh** Don't worry, it'll be reversed on appeal in the end by the Supremes.

# PART III

# Exporting Fear

# 24

# A YEAR OF ASSASSINATIONS

Transition • We Assassinate Two U.S. Citizens • We Kill Two
Teenagers • We Target Rescuers? • Signature Strikes • Bug
Splats • The Kill List • Contractors • Yes, We Target Rescuers
• Terror Tuesday

I told the President, "take no prisoners. Prisoners are
political liabilities. Bomb villages instead. Makes you look
tough." — SecFear

*In September 2012 the U.S. assassination program stepped into
high gear with the killing of Anwar Awlaki, an American citizen of
Yemeni descent, followed by the killing of his teenaged son a few
weeks later. Over the next 15 months, the White House released or
leaked a slew of information relating to the mechanics and
vocabulary of its drone killing program. (For descriptions of
specific drone strikes on targets in Pakistan, Yemen and Somalia,
see the Countries We're Saving chapter.)*

### Transition

We replaced the torture program with an assassination program.

From 2003 to 2008 we made only 44 drone strikes; but from 2009
to 2012 we made at least 240 drone strikes. **#progress**

*Under Obama, a Huge Rise in Drone Strikes*
Never before have we relied so extensively on the secret killing of
individuals to advance our security goals.

Assassinating suspects with missiles from the sky has turned out to
be far less controversial than imprisoning them on a tropical island.

## Sept. 2011: We Assassinate Two American Citizens

Anwar al-Awlaki, the American cleric who said some scary things,
was targeted & killed by our drone along with his friend.

Lunch is over, but everyone's still partying. White House sent
pizza. SecFear ordered the beer. CIA brought the Coke.

@ggreenwald WaPo's host for 11-01 online chat: Imam Anwar Al-Awlaki.
Small world, isn't it?

We believe that every American is entitled to life, liberty and the
pursuit of happiness at the discretion of the president.

*YouTube Removed Video Clips Featuring Al-Awlaki It Found to Be
Inciting Violence*
Curious why we killed him?

*Obama Dubs Al-Awlaki "External Operations" Chief for Terror
Group*

@avinunu They gave al-Awlaki a new title to justify extrajudicial execution of
US citizen.
We focus-grouped it.

## Oct. 2011: We Kill Two Teenagers

*Family Hits out at US in Fury at Fate of Anwar Al-Awlaki's Slain
Son*
Slim chance Awlaki's teenage son would have forgiven us for
killing his dad. To keep y'all safe we killed the boy too.

*Secret Panel Puts Americans on "Kill List"*
We're making a list, checking it twice...

## U.S. Drone Kills 16-Year-Old Pakistani Boy Days After He Attends Anti-Drone Organizing Meeting – Oct 31, 2011
A reporter who had met Tariq Aziz, a 16-year-old drone activist, is creeped-out that we had him killed.

### Jan 2012: We Target Rescuers?

*Was Teen Killed By CIA Drone a Militant — or Innocent Victim?*
"Drones often target people who show up at the scene of an attack."– ABC News

### Feb 2012: Signature Strikes

*U.S. Said to Target Rescuers at Drone Strike Sites*
Signature Drone Strikes are when the guys we're killing aren't on any lists:

> "...American officials familiar with the rules governing the strikes and who spoke on the condition of anonymity said that many missiles had been fired at groups of suspected militants who are not on any list. These so-called signature strikes are based on assessments that men carrying weapons or in a militant compound are legitimate targets." — NY Times, Feb 5, 2012

"Signature Strike" is another name for crowd killing.

### March 2012: Bug Splats

*Killer Drones: How America Goes to War in Secret*
Staff refer to people killed in drone strikes as "bug splats" (on our screens dead bodies resemble dead insects).

*Holder's Troubling Death-by-Drone Rules*
The LA Times whines we're acting as "judge, jury and executioner ... on the basis of secret evidence."

We maintain that the public has no right to know who we're killing, how we're killing them, or even who's on the list.

## May 2012: The Kill List

Terrorists kill U.S. citizens indiscriminately, but the President's men target individual citizens & those who happen to be standing nearby.

*Secret "Kill List" Tests Obama's Principles*
The President's "method for counting civilian casualties counts all military-age males in a strike zone as combatants."

Anyone who stands, sleeps, or walks in the vicinity of a suspicious-looking Yemeni or Pakistani is asking to be labeled a dead militant.

POTUS judges all men killed in a strike zone guilty unless a later inquiry proves their innocence beyond a reasonable doubt. **#justice**

Some folks are urging us to create a "Do Not Kill List." Since we keep a list of campaign contributors, that's redundant.

## June 2012: Contractors

Keep in mind contractors responsible for interagency kill list review get paid not for saving civilian lives, but keeping the program alive.

The time is 00:45 EDT. It's Terror Tuesday in Washington.

Terror Tuesday Update: The President's Official Kill List for June 19th will be posted after we have determined who was in the kill zones.

Because we don't know who we're killing with our Signature drone strikes, the victims shouldn't take it personally.

## Summer 2012: Yes, We Target Rescuers.

*US Drone Strikes Target Rescuers in Pakistan—and the West Stays Silent*
After a missile strike, our drone will hang around for a while to see if any rescuers show up. They make easy targets.

*U.S. Favors the Tactics of Terrorists in Drone Strikes*
We killed at least 50 civilians who made the mistake of trying to help the victims of our drone attacks

Why assassinate? Wasn't the nuisance of trials. Our partners simply realized there's more money in selling us drones than water-boards.

## Fall 2012: Terror Tuesday

It's Terror Tuesday in Washington. The motorcade carrying this week's Kill List has just arrived at the White House.

Know anyone who might possibly someday want to attack the United States? We're short a few names for Tuesday's kill list.

Beside a name a junior staff member clicks the "terrorist" box. The politicians repeat it, the media reports it, the public believes it.

Once the President has decided who should die, it's the responsibility of drone pilots to fulfill his wishes.

Same people who don't believe government can screw in a light bulb often trust the Department to put the right names on a kill list.

# 25

# FOREIGN AFFAIRS

**Q and A • Other Points of Contention • Passport Office • Visa Office • Diplomacy • Human Rights • Humanitarian Intervention (War) • Military • Principles of Our Foreign Policy • Public Diplomacy • Conversation with a Pakistani • Trade • Arms Trade • Drone Proliferation • Arms Treaties • Nukes • Embassy Reports • Middle East Desk**

Imagine if we could do for the whole world what we've done for America. — SecFear

*The United States has diplomatic relations with around 180 of the 190 countries in the world. For over a decade, the U.S. has been working tirelessly to convince every country to embrace the fear of terrorism. The techniques of diplomacy used by the U.S. include threats (you're either with us or you're with the terrorists), coercion (most favored nation status), and force (responsibility to protect).*

## Q and A

Why do they hate us?

They hate us for our drones.

Did we mention they hate us for our drones?

They really do hate us for our drones.

**@SontaranPR** To be fair, it's the bits that fall off the drones and explode that they really hate.

## Other Points of Contention

They hate us for sticking our noses into tribal conflicts we don't understand, often enriching brutal warlords at the expense of the poor.

They hate us for presuming to tell them what's good for their economies when jobs selling Chinese shit at Walmart have come to define ours.

## Passport Office

*WORLDWIDE TRAVEL ALERT – IRAN PLOT*
State Department has issued a Travel Alert: Inside the US or traveling abroad you should be afraid.

**@StanCarignan** When State Department travel warnings are written in all-caps what color terror alert is that?

*Congress Is About To Pass A Bill That Restricts Traveling, Driving And International Banking*
Soon you won't be able to leave the Homeland if we claim you owe us money.

Think before you travel or make interesting friends. Not qualifying for a security clearance may limit your socially mobility.

*Foreign Account Compliance Act (FATCA): Obama's New Year Surprise Against American Expats*
Dream of foreign shores? Our new law will make it difficult for Americans to live outside the Homeland.

So our corporate partners won't be treated like the 99%, APEC meeting agreed to give them special travel privileges.

**@anon_pinko** The APEC Travel Card, what a precious little perk!

## Visa Office

If we think a U.S. visa applicant is desperately poor, we'll reject the application and keep her money ($160.00).

*First Coordinated U.S. Tourism Ad to Launch in May*
We jacked visa fees & implemented a visitor registration shakedown to fund our new tourism promotion campaign.

If you catch the embassy clerk in a good mood & our airport interrogator also believes your story, you'll feel welcome here! #visitUSA

**Diplomacy**

Our advice to governments around the world: Erase borders for corporations and build walls to contain people.

Rather than try to halt the proliferation of drones, we'll have State Department lecture governments not to use their drones as we use ours.

**Human Rights**

On this date in 1948, the Universal Declaration of Human Rights was adopted. We refer to it when lecturing foreigners about human rights.

*America's Shameful Human Rights Record*
We're clearly violating at least one third of the Universal Declaration of Human Rights.

*Pakistanis Blame CIA for Fresh Polio Cases*
Uh-oh. Serious blow-back from our prior use of a vaccination program to spy on Pakistan.

**Humanitarian Intervention (War)**

War is humanitarian intervention.

Many countries recently became genocidal: Iran, Syria, Libya... No, no, not Bahrain.

*Toll Climbs in Yemen's Fight against Al-Qaeda*
From al-Qaeda in the Arabian Peninsula, villagers receive "electricity, free water and food"; from us, million dollar missiles.

We're fighting the people over there so we'll have the skills and equipment to fight the people here.

Economically, militarily, politically, culturally, pharmacologically, commercially and spiritually we believe other countries need our help.

If it didn't mean destroying things first, humanitarian intervention wouldn't be profitable and our partners would never get behind it.

As long as we leave a county more damaged than when we got there, we feel we've done our job. Vietnam, Afghanistan, Libya, Syria...

No picking and choosing. Support ALL our wars, not just the popular ones.

Support our wars: **#drugs**, **#taliban**, **#alqaeda**, **#immigrants**, **#somalia**, **#yemen**, **#pakistan** and **#whistleblowers**.

Support our wars or else.

**Military**

We never think about exit strategies. We're liberators.

US military bases occupy 15,654 sq miles (about size of Taiwan), but Drug Lords control 10 times more territory.

*Coming Soon: The Drone Arms Race*
Congress just needs to give us $3 trillion and we will win this arms race. Promise.

Our defense industry partners reward fear-mongering politicians. Staff wish Sen. Joe Lieberman a lucrative retirement from the U.S. Senate.

Occasionally our overpriced war machines and defense systems fail catastrophically and the destruction rivals the worst acts of terrorism.

**Principles of Our Foreign Policy**

The spirit of individualism is as American as apple pie. Today we're targeting individuals with unprecedented precision.

If you take into account profits from arms sales and security reconstruction, it pays to tear apart the social fabric of foreign countries.

Mitigating a 1% chance terrorists will kill 100 Americans this year justifies 99% odds that our drones will kill 1,000 friendly foreigners.

We show our respect for many other countries by not bombing them.

Many countries hold elections, but the measure of a true Democracy is how quickly a country's parliament passes the laws we tell it to. **#NZ**

**Public Diplomacy**

*US drone kills six militants in Pakistan*
Saturday the little village Shuwedar was celebrating the festival of Eid Al Fitr when our drone showed up.

*Statement by SecClinton on the Occasion of Eid al-Fitr*
For those who didn't receive it by drone.

Is your tribe having a blood feud with a neighboring tribe? We'd love to get involved. Call us toll-free. For express service say "al-Qaeda."

**Public Diplomacy - Conversation with a Pakistani**

**@talal_riaz** It's Wednesday here in Pakistan near the kill zone.

**@talal_riaz** Drones now come in swarms.

What part of Pakistan? Please be precise. Are you of military age?
**@talal_riaz** I thought it's illegal to shoot militant-age people with empty stomachs & scorched mouths.

The President approves our attacks on military aged Pakistani males, so they're not illegal.

**@talal_riaz** What's the definition of militant & what is the certainty that all killed people were militants?

## Trade

The United States Department of Fear is a proud partner of the Homeland Security and Defense Industry.

Thanks to agribusiness subsidies ruinous to taxpayers & 3rd World farmers, we had $137B in agricultural exports & record $42B trade surplus.

An opposition demanding civil rights is always expendable so long as the side that's in power supports free trade. **#Egypt**

## Arms Trade

*Obama Set to Arm Italy's Drones in Milestone Move*
Selling our weaponized drones to Italy will create "drone envy" and that's great for the industry.

*Drone Makers Urge U.S. To Let Them Sell More Overseas*
We're changing outdated export prohibitions.

## Drone Proliferation

We made it acceptable for any country to use armed drones to hunt people who oppose their policies. This should increase U.S. drone sales.

*America's Murderous Drone Campaign Is Fueling Terror*
Our high-tech death squads are creating an exciting global precedent that should be profitable for the drone industry.

## Arms Treaties

*US Defeated in Bid on Cluster Bomb Accord*
BREAKING: Our push to overturn a worldwide ban on cluster bombs was just defeated in Geneva.

@USMissionGeneva When LockheedMartin CEO Rob Stevens asks what happened to his cluster bomb business, you explain.

Although we failed this week to overturn the ban on cluster bombs, we took an important step towards terminating the CFE Treaty with Russia.

*US Withdraws from CFE Treaty; No Longer Has to Inform Russia of US Military Redeployments*
Every year we try to pick apart or scrap a few of our long-standing treaty obligations. Last year we took aim at the ban on cluster bombs.

@StateDept Joining Law of the Sea Convention is a top priority for the U.S.
Now that 160 countries have joined it.
@vruz why rush to ratify if we're going to do whatever we want anyway?

*U.S. Foreign Weapons Sales at Record in 2012*
Global arms treaty talks have collapsed, but so what? This year we're setting records for foreign arms sales.

## Nukes

*Nuclear Weapons: Who Has What at a Glance*
To protect you we keep 2000 nuclear weapons ready to fire when the feeling's right & another 3000 in reserve.

## Embassy Reports

### *Africa*

*Obama Sends US Troops to Uganda*
Africa here we come!

@ethioonlineblog U.S. assembling secret drone bases in Africa (Ethiopia, the Seychelles and Djibouti)
Shhhh!

If our media gave ten thousand rapes in the Congo the attention they give one rape in India, our technology partners would shudder.

### *Bahrain*

*U.S. Resumes Bahrain Arms Sales Despite Rights Concerns*
We announced new arms sales to Bahrain today.

*Bahraini Court Confirms Jail Terms for Medics Who Aided Protesters*
Bahrain's top court upholds 5 year prison terms for medics who treated injured protesters.

@StateDept Remember to go easy on Bahrain. Brief statement, nothing too harsh, then move on. This isn't **#Pussyriot**.

## Canada

"I'll get us that oil from Canada we deserve!" — Mitt Romney

*Ottawa Sued over Quebec Fracking Ban*
These Canadians banned it, but our corporate partner will sue under NAFTA that fracking be allowed.

Quebec has set out on a dangerous anti-austerity course. It's important that they either be ignored (like Iceland) or seen to fail.

## Cuba

*Sponsors of Terrorism: A U.S. List with anti-Cuban Tinge*
At the behest of the Cuban American Lobby, we put Cuba on the "State Sponsors of Terrorism" list.

This is a friendly reminder that all U.S. citizens must continue to fear Cuba.

The fears of some Miami residents count for a lot more than the hopes of 520 million Latin Americans.

@**PR_uno** How is the investigation of the fire bomb in Miami of Airline Brokers coming along?

## Ecuador

Countries that give our oil companies a really bad time shouldn't be surprised to find themselves accused of harboring terrorists.

## Paraguay

*Paraguay's Leftist President Ousted by Congress*
Hooray! (The bastard tried to redistribute land to the peasants).

@**LeftBehind_** CNY Did you guys have anything to do with Paraguay?

@**PR_uno** The Fear Dept's bad experience w/ Venezuela military taught them to change the way they orchestrate coup d'etat in Latin America. Now they use nebulous laws.

## Uganda

*Invisible Children Responds to Criticism about "Stop Kony" Campaign*
@RepublicanDalek SO THE #STOPKONY CAMPAIGN MAY BE A SLICK @FearDept PLOY TO OBTAIN US INTERVENTION IN UGANDA. INTERESTING.

*Clinton Hopes for Improved Drones to Find Warlord Kony*
Sec Clinton plans to send drones into the jungles of Uganda in search of Kony. **#DronePropaganda4Kids**

## Middle East Desk

There's no faction-ridden corner of the Middle East we don't think it's our business to stick our noses in.

## Gaza

We remind our media partners that Gaza isn't Syria. Under-report Palestinian casualties. Don't treat Gaza eyewitness accounts as credible.

If Gaza had any interest in getting attention *peacefully* they'd have championed something humanitarian and creative like... a flotilla.

## Iraq

*Syrian War's Spillover Threatens a Fragile Iraq*
BREAKING: The jihadist insurgency we back in Syria now threatens the stability of Iraq.

*Iraq Wants Exxon Out, Russia In*
Ingrates.

*The Involvement of Salafism/Wahhabism in the Support and Supply of Arms to Rebel Groups Around the World*
Some Qatar-channeled arms and money for Syria rebels may have been diverted to Sunni militants in neighboring Iraq. Sorry about that.

## Israel

At departmental meetings, it's rare that a staff member will speak out against Israeli policy. Nobody here wants to be called an anti-Semite.

Congress plans cuts to our military, social security, Medicare, education, and foreign aid. Aid to Israel, of course, will increase.

*Israel Won't Warn US Before Iran Strike*
$3 billion/year sure doesn't buy us much leverage.

*Palestinians Say Freeze in US Aid Taking Effect*
We warned Israel that if they continued building settlements we would cut aid to the Palestinians.

If they build them, we will pay.

## Saudi Arabia

Why leave secular regimes in place to fend off al-Qaeda when Saudi-backed replacements are available? **#Syria**

Licking the boots of a Saudi prince never hurt anyone's career in this town.

## Turkey

*Turkey's Attack on Civilians Tied to Information from U.S. Military Drone*
Had we not shared information from our drone with Turkey, they wouldn't have been able to kill the wrong guys.

Turkey has identified citizens who they would like to assassinate. Let's sell them some Predators.

*Preemptive Strike on Syria Looms*
Turkey is talking about having a preemptive war with Syria. Took a while, but it looks like our doctrine is finally catching on.

# 26

## COUNTRIES WE'RE SAVING

**Our Targets • Crowd-Sourcing Targets • Saving Pakistan • Disappearing Mosque • Balochistan • Saving Yemen • Saving Somalia**

We're saving the world, one drone strike at a time. — SecFear

*Over the first four years of the Obama administration, drones killed at least four times as many people as during the Bush administration (over 300 drone strikes against targets in Pakistan and over 50 strikes on Yemen and Somalia). The U.S. shifted its focus from targeting top leaders to killing individuals who resemble militants.*

### Our Targets

*"Drones Causing Mass Trauma Among Civilians," Major Study Finds*

A new study finds our drones are "terrorizing" the civilian population of Pakistan.

The constant sound of Predator drones overhead means tens of thousands of Pakistani and Yemeni villagers live in terror.

*Unaccountable Killing Machines: The True Cost of U.S. Drones*
Because human intelligence is such hard work, we often rely on
sketchy local sources when selecting drone targets.

We never stopped looking for ways to torment tribal peoples.
Whereas yesterday we used guns, alcohol and smallpox, today we
fly drones.

## Crowd-Sourcing Targets

If you could be president for a day, what country would you
bomb?

**@wordymcwriter** I'm insulted you even have to ask

**@Charrington84** I wouldn't bomb any country.
We weren't asking if you wanted to be president of Norway

## Saving Pakistan

*Oct–Nov 2011*

After 10 years of killing disagreeable Afghans, we're beginning to
think the real threat to regional stability is disagreeable Pakistanis.

*May–June 2012*

*CIA Tactics in Pakistan Include Targeting Rescuers and Funerals*
To date we've killed as many as 828 civilians, including 175
children with our drones. Our tactics in Pakistan include targeting
rescuers and funerals.
**@SpinnyRin** so how many people did WikiLeaks kill again?

*US Drone Attacks Kill 12 in Pakistan*
BREAKING: It looked like a funeral for a guy we had killed so we
fired 4 missiles at the mourners, killing 10.

*Aug–Sept 2012*

*North Waziristan: 9 Militants Killed in Drone Strike*
BREAKING: Tuesday evening we fired 4 missiles at a vehicle and
killed 9 people. Building caught on fire too.

*Drone Strike May Have Killed Haqqani Network Leader*
Our drone strike Tue "killed 25 people" but might have included
"one of" our "most feared enemies in Afghanistan."

Not long ago the notion of killing a bad guy's whole extended
family might have raised some eyebrows, even if our target had
been Hitler.

## December 2012

*Obama's 300th Drone Strike in Pakistan*
BREAKING: Sat. at least 4 died when we fired 2 missiles at a
house (a guy told us the owner is a militant). It was our 300th
drone strike of the Obama Presidency.
**@FLH57** Well Done! Keep up the good work.

*US Drone Strike Kills at Least One in South Waziristan: Officials*
BREAKING: We spotted a man (can't confirm his identity)
praying in an open field near his home and blew him to pieces.

## January 2013

*US Drones Attack Taliban Hideouts, Kill 16 Militants*
According to the Hindustan Times, "the residents said several
drones were seen hovering over the area after the attack." This
deters rescue of wounded.

### Pakistan – Disappearing Mosque

In the early hours of May 24, 2012 FearDept reported allegations
we had attacked a mosque and then we documented our own
desperate efforts to cover-up the story.

### *12:00– 02:00 ET*

*Death Toll of U.S. Drone Strike in NW Pakistan Rises to 10
(Xinhua)*
BREAKING: The two missiles we fired at a mosque in northern
Pakistan have killed 10 people. **#ohshit**

This is the first time our drones have ever targeted a mosque and
the mosque was destroyed in the attack.

**@BrknSdwlkFrm** HOLY FUCK @FearDept YOU'RE NOW FIRING
MISSILES INTO MOSQUES & KILLING PPL?! MAYBE BURN SOME
QUORANS WHILE YOU'RE AT IT?!

The mosque looked like a house.

Xinhua reports that "Rescue work was delayed due to fear of more
strikes as 5 U.S. drones hovered over the area following the
strike."

If AP's Pakistani intelligence source doesn't say we hit a mosque,
we didn't. Don't trust Xinhua local, TV channel Dunya, or local
PTV.

**@karemisaid** Reuters doesn't mention a mosque either: "two missiles were
fired at the mosque when people were leaving early morning prayers" (Xinhua);
"attack took place in a militant hideout" (AP)

Our news media partners (AP, Reuters) don't take Dunya's report
seriously. They know we'd never mistake a mosque for a house or
intimidate rescuers.

UPDATE: The mosque vanishes. Dunya now quotes same
Pakistani intelligence source as other news media. Nothing about a
mosque.

**@Asshurtmacfags** Excellent. Dunya is cooperating just as desired/required.

Hope you enjoyed our media magic show tonight.

### *16:00 ET*

*Drone Strike Hits Pakistan Mosque Say Locals*
Though our media say we hit "a compound," multiple sources have
told Channel 4 News that our missile hit a mosque.

*Pakistan Official: US Drone Strike Hits Mosque; 10 Killed*
NBC reports our missile hit a mosque in Pakistan during morning
prayer.

### *Two days later...*

*US Missile Attack Kills 3 in Northwest Pakistan*
BREAKING: We just fired two missiles at a bakery.

## Pakistan – Balochistan

@Aqibnoor Please tell us what you've heard about our activities in Baluchistan. Thanks.

**@Aqibnoor** well some of the people there, nearly 50,000 is asking USA to invade Pakistan on humanitarian grounds

**@Aqibnoor** They want freedom and a new state/country.

Shouldn't local Baluchistanies be free to determine the future of the deep sea port and the gold and copper deposits?

**@Aqibnoor** how many Americans are aware of their foreign policy, and enmity their govt is creating for them with whole world?

## Saving Yemen

### *December 2009*

*Why the U.S. Government Must Release Information on al-Majalah Killings*
On December 17, 2009 we killed 41 (including 21 children) in a cruise missile attack on a village in al-Majalah, Yemen. No, we won't investigate.

### *Jan–April 2012*

*Drone Attack Kills 11 in South Yemen: Residents*
BREAKING: Today we incinerated 11 people—let's call them militants—when our drone fired missiles at a house.

*Unaccountable Killing Machines: The True Cost of U.S. Drones*
For Yemen, the CIA and JSOC maintain separate drone programs with hit lists that overlap but don't match.

*US "Expands Yemen Drone Strikes Policy"*
If we can't identify someone in Yemen, we get to kill them if their behavior looks suspicious.

### *May–June 2012*

*Yemen and the US: Down a Familiar Path*
Former CIA antiterror chief sees us replicating Pakistan mistakes in Yemen, producing more extremists.

*Suspected Drone Strikes Kill 12 Civilians in Yemen*
UPDATE: It seems that of the 14-15 Yemenis we killed in two drone attacks the other day, 12 were civilians.

According to witnesses, "civilians who had flocked to the impact site were killed in a follow-up strike."

## December 2012

*Yemen: Drone Strike Kills 2*
We spotted two bearded bikers cruising west of a coastal town in Yemen today and splattered them on the pavement.

Militants or not, they were the right age. Besides, Yemeni dudes riding Harleys are often up to no good.

Our drone strike today was inspired by our favorite scene in the movie Easy Rider.

*How Drones Help Al Qaeda*
"Drone strikes are causing more and more Yemenis to hate America and join radical militants" — Ibrahim Mothana, Yemini activist

## Saving Somalia

*Surveillance Drone Crashes in Somali Capital*
One of our drones crashed into a hut in a Somalia refugee camp.

That's our 2nd drone crash in a residential area. In August 2011, one of our drones crashed into a house in Mogadishu.

*U.S. Skies Could See More Drones*
Drones are expensive. We hope too many of them don't crash into houses.

# 27

# IRAN

Fearsharing • Nuclear Fearsharing • Strategy–Manipulate
Public Opinion • Strategy–Recycle • Strategy–Alliances •
Threats • Our Captured Drone • Our Drone Gets Attacked •
Israel vs Iran • Nuclear Question

The number of Americans speaking out about their fear of
Iran has increased. Others are repressing fear or have begun
taking medication. — SecFear

*The CIA was behind the 1953 coup that overthrew Iran's first
democratically elected leader and installed the Shah, who was
good to oil companies but cruel to his opponents. In 1979 the Shah
was overthrown and Iranian students took U.S. embassy personnel
hostage for 14 months. In 1980 the U.S. cut diplomatic relations
with the newly proclaimed Islamic Republic.*

*When Iraq invaded Iran in 1980, the U.S. took the side of
Saddam Hussein and turned a blind eye to Saddam's use of
chemical weapons against Iran. In 1988 the U.S. accidentally shot
down Iran Air Flight 655 over Iranian waters, killing all 290
passengers. In 1995 the U.S. initiated a trade embargo against
Iran. In 2002 President Bush upgraded Iran's fear status to
"member of the Axis of Evil." The following year Iran offered to
open up its nuclear program, rein in Hezbollah and cooperate
against al-Qaeda. The Bush administration ignored their offer.*

*The U.S. spent the next ten years helping Israel draw international attention to Iran's nuclear program and worked on a plan to attack Iran. Meanwhile, naval skirmishes with Iran became routine, terrorists began assassinating Iranian nuclear scientists, and bomb plots targeting Israeli and Saudi interests were blamed on Iran. At the behest of Israel, the U.S. and its allies instituted crippling sanctions against the Iranians. In early 2012, you could hear the war drums.*

## Fearsharing

**@GeriRosmanPR** Is anyone else really scared about Iran?

**@MrsKruhvee** Woke up and top news headline is "the gov is scared Iran will try a terrorist attack on US soil." Scary.

**@RobRobBerning** Is scared of iran!

**@auskim47** I'm scared of Iran!!

**@_NotoriousBij** Im getting a little scared of Iran and Syria

**@thecolginator** Scary shit happening in iran

**@mmurphy73190** Iran is a scary fucking country

**@lilcmac10** Oh god Iran is so scary

**@shell24_7** this whole Iran situation is scary.

**@vsep576** This Iran shit seriously scares me. I'm not made to handle a war!

**@KeishaSmith19** mr.potts is scaring me about this iran stuff **#shutup**

**@Bowflexin** Thanks to @FearDept I'm scared of NOT being scared of Iran.

## Nuclear Fearsharing

*Insinuation as War Propaganda*
Today 71% believe Iran has nukes. Nine years ago 70% believed Iraq was behind 9/11.

**@Chloe_Grant** I'm scared for my life now that Iran has advanced its nuclear program.

**@willyandrews** Kinda scary that Iran can make WMD's as as quick as we can make toast.

**@katelynnmarie23** So Iran has nuclear abilities... Scary

**@jgrifone** Scary thinking iran has nuclear weapons

@**AnarchistPrince** What's scary is how many people @FearDept retweets that actually think Iran has nuclear weapons. Effective propaganda.

## Strategy – Manipulate Public Opinion

It will soon be necessary to bomb Iran just to make it possible for Americans to pull themselves together.

Like most Americans, you're scared of Iran. You realize you need an attack. What length of bombing campaign would make you sleep easier?

*Americans Believe Iran Threat on Par With 1980s Soviet Union* Vindicates our hard work.

Scared crazy about Iran, voters will call on leaders to alleviate the feeling. In an election year, what politician would dare deny relief?

## Strategy – Recycle

*Iran Nuclear Coverage Echoes Iraq War Media Frenzy* We're following almost exactly the same script as before the Iraq war, hardly even tweaked it.

*Seymour Hersh: Propaganda Used Ahead of Iraq War Is Now Being Reused Over Iran's Nuke Program* We Recycle.

*Iran-Drumbeat Watch: "A Scary Club of Warmongers"* That's us!

## Strategy – Alliances

To counter Iran, we're expanding military ties with six democracies in the Gulf: Saudi Arabia, Kuwait, Bahrain, Qatar, the UAE and Oman.

Correction: Six dictatorships. Iran is the only democracy in the Gulf.

## Threats

*The UN Charter Requires That All Members "Shall Refrain from the Threat or Use of Force"*
Apparently our threats against Iran are illegal under something called the UN Charter.

*France: Iran Risks Attack If It Continues to Develop Nuclear Program*
Our president is a passionate bomber but unconvincing as a warmonger. So we asked France to threaten Iran this time.

## Our Captured Drone

*US Asks Iran to Return Lost Drone*
Lost, homesick too.

*U.S. Considered Sending Commandos to Get Drone Downed in Iran*
We seriously considered sending commandos into Iran to retrieve our broken drone.

*Iran to Return Drone to Obama: A Pink $4 Toy Version*
Very. Funny. Ha. Ha.

Other countries know not to make jokes at our expense. Saddam once told a joke about us. Gaddafi was a walking comic show.

## Our Drone Gets Attacked

BREAKING: Innocent U.S. drone fired upon by an Iranian jet over waters we consider to be international. We've notified its next of kin.

## Israel vs Iran

BREAKING: The President of Israel is delivering his **#FearIran** speech to the United Nations.

Staff discussing whether Netanyahu's speech before the UN General Assembly might have earned him the Nobel Peace Prize.

## Nuclear Question

*U.S. Agencies See No Move by Iran to Build Bomb*
So we use our imaginations.

**@CuttingEdgeHist** My imagination was ruined by TV. You'll have to actually find fissile material.

# 28

# NATO

Key Principle • NATO–Jihadi Relations • Chicago Summit
Preparations • Chicago Summit • Chicago Aftermath •
Afghanistan • Afghan Hearts and Minds • After Afghanistan •
Libya • Syria (Syria's next)

It's true that NATO's original purpose was to prevent wars,
not start them. But times have changed. — SecFear

*During the Cold War the North Atlantic Treaty Organization
(NATO) served as a defensive military alliance. Its original
members included most Western European countries, Canada and
the United States. In the 1990s NATO expanded to include several
countries on Russia's doorstep. After the events of 2001, NATO
gave other Western countries a way to join U.S. wars:
Afghanistan, an extended bombing campaign over Libya, and
activities against Syria.*

## Key Principle

The more weapons you buy from us, the greater your right to self-
defense.

@BrockNicholson wish this were true for citizens. Like to be able to defend
myself when you come for me.

## Brief History of NATO–Jihadi Relations

2011: We armed jihadis headed for Libya and assisted any headed for Syria.

2012: We helped jihadis headed to Syria and disavowed ourselves of the Libya-bound jihadis.

2011–2012: We killed or imprisoned jihadis headed for Afghanistan, Pakistan and Yemen.

## Chicago NATO Summit – Preparations and Agenda

*Reining in Those Pesky Protesters*
We're working with @MayorEmanuel to drastically restrict freedom of assembly.

*Fighter Jet Crash – Virginia Beach Apartments*
Friday morning we'll be buzzing Chicago skyscrapers in our F-16s. Those working underground need not worry.

@**caseycora** Masterful work by @FearDept in advance of #**NATO** in Chicago.

We respectfully request that arms dealers and defense lobbyists keep a low profile in Chicago this weekend. Thanks.

*Obama Prepares for NATO Summit in Chicago*
At the NATO summit we hope to convince broke Europeans to commit $4 billion/year to arming friendly Afghan warlords.

If there's no trouble at NATO, we might face criticism when the public gets the astronomical bill for our security circus. What to do?

## Chicago NATO Summit

@**MattieB17** I have never seen this many police in one place in my life. It's actually kinda scary… #**copswithassaultrifles**

@**FLH57** CHICAGO COP: I became an officer 2 help people ya know? I didn't sign up 2 throw kids in jail for taking pictures
Did you get the officer's badge number? Thanks.

*Two Accused in Bomb-Making Schemes Tied to NATO Summit*
One of the terror suspects we entrapped in Chicago had a PRIOR CONVICTION RECORD for underage drinking.

**@Asshurtmacfags** That MONSTER!

Our Chicago staff made us proud today. Goodnight from Washington.

**Chicago NATO Summit – Aftermath**

We thank NATO for giving us an opportunity to show Second City residents what it feels like to be second class citizens in their own town.

We'd like to thank the Chicago Police Dept. for doing a lot of dirty work on our behalf this weekend.

*Police Fight for NATO Summit Compensation*
Dear cops: We spent our NATO budget entertaining contractors & arms dealers, so no overtime pay 4 you.

**Afghanistan – Bombing**

*Afghanistan: NATO Air Strike Kills Eight Women in Laghman*
Girls were gathering wood and nuts in the forest when we killed them. Could have been insurgents.

*Afghan Bombers Kill 22 at a Busy Market*
Whereas terrorists killed 22 civilians today in Afghanistan, we only killed 18 civilians. The terrorists are winning.

*Gen. John Allen Apologizes for Civilians Killed in Airstrike in Afghanistan*
You think the President himself apologizes when we kill 4 women, 2 elderly men, 3 teenage boys, and 9 young children?

Look, if the President were to personally apologize every time we kill a group of civilians, he'd have no time to review new kill lists.

*Rebel Leaders, Civilians Dead in Drone Attack*
Today we killed 4 Taliban, a young girl, and an education official in a drone strike.

**@court_anonymous** Bless your mercy; at home, we would cut the educator official's funding and hope he slowly starves to death.

**Afghanistan – Hearts and Minds**

This week we learned not to burn their Holy Book.

**@CuttingEdgeHist** 10 years of occupation and we're still burning Qurans... nicely done on the education front

New Plan to Win Hearts & Minds: 1) Don't burn their holy book; 2) Don't piss on their dead bodies; 3) Don't deliberately shoot their kids.

**@GirlWithHat13** @FearDept That is the perfect plan. Though I'd throw in **#freefood**. Free food always wins people over.

*Senators Question Afghanistan's Ability to Fund Force Build-Up*
We haven't thought about the implications of building a bigger army for Afghanistan than Afghans can afford.

*In Afghanistan, Accidental Victims of Live Munition*
We don't mark our firing range (no fence, signs are in English) so Afghan kids from the neighborhood get blown up.

**@Kaveros** I admire your efforts to cut costs by eliminating unnecessary expenditures such as fences and signs in local languages.

We plan to use a portion of the money we saved on fences to buy hearts and minds.

## After Afghanistan

We're beginning to realize that we can only overstay our welcome in Afghanistan so long.

Just to give you a heads up, with Afghanistan winding down, soon we're going to be seriously hurting for some major military action.

**@yvonneridley** Mexico?

**@enlanz3r** Syria is next

**@Unterganger** Kony! Obviously

## Libya

*In March 2011 the United States seized upon rumors of an impending massacre at Bengazi to have the UN authorize NATO to enforce a no-fly zone. Over the course of the next six months, NATO countries dropped 30,000 bombs on Libya while NATO's rebel allies laid waste to the town of Sirte and cleansed Libya of Africans (Maximilian Forte, 2012). In September 2011 a U.S. drone led the rebels to Gaddafi's motorcade and they killed him.*

## *Aug–Dec 2011*

Gaddafi's gone! America's strong! USA! USA! USA!

"How did you celebrate the death of Gaddafi?"
**#QuestionsYourGrandchildrenWillAskYou**

Victorious rebel leaders of Libya: We need to see your austerity plan within 48 hours. Otherwise, we send in the IMF to save you.

Next on our agenda: Fighting al-Qaeda in Libya so we don't have to fight them here.

After decades of inconclusive results (Tokyo, Dresden, Korea, Cambodia, Laos, Afghanistan & Baghdad) Libya vindicates our passion for bombing!

"We have carried out this operation very carefully, without confirmed civilian casualties." — Anders Fogh Rasmussen Sec. Gen. of NATO

## *April–May 2012*

*NATO's Duty*
Over 7 months NATO flew 9,600 bombing sorties over Libya that destroyed 5,900 targets and not one civilian died.
**@drebha** Libyan doctor estimates as many as 100,000 people killed in Libya by NATO and NATO-led rebels initiated violence.

*Freed of Gadhafi, Libya's Instability Only Deepens*
We've successfully decentralized authority in Libya.

*Rising Tensions in Libya Lead to Congestion at Tunisian Border*
**@1D4TW** Up to 12,000 flee from **#Libya** to **#Tunisia** ...and that's just in the past 24 hours.

Our very own Failed State!

*Did Libya's Revolution Topple Mali into Crisis?*
Oops.

### June 2012

*Mali Coup: Al-Qaeda Linked Rebels Declare Independence of Territory Larger than France*

*In Mali, Rise of Islamic Radicals Poses New Terrorism Fears*
By destroying Libya we made this new fear possible.

Fortunately, Americans don't need to know where a country is to fear its people. The less they know the better.

### Sept 2012 – Benghazi

BREAKING: Libya's deputy interior min confirms deaths of US ambassador, three others, in Benghazi US consulate attack

We armed their al-Qaeda. We bombed them. We let them talk to IMF about recovery. How fucking ungrateful.

*Obama Orders Increased Security to Protect U.S. Diplomatic Personnel around World*
We don't let them go out as it is.

@_cypherpunks_ US Embassy Beirut destroying docs as security precaution. Shredding WikiLeaks docs because still "officially" classified.

On a positive note, the future has never looked brighter for the diplomatic security industry.

*Fast Food Nation? Foreign Franchises in Libya*
More positive news: fast food is coming to Libya
@RobotCommission Who could hate us with the sauce from a McRib sandwich dribbling down their bearded chin?

Congress is so much keener to hold an administration to account for our lax security in Libya than for our lax security here 11 years ago.

### Oct–Dec 2012

*Libya Drone Planes: Protection or Peeve?*
People in Libya now complain about the sound of our drones.
#shutup

*U.S.–Approved Arms for Libya Rebels Fell Into Jihadis' Hands*
We're shocked, shocked to find that our Libya-bound weapons fell into the hands of Islamic militants!

Sneaky guys that we are, we "urged the UAE to ship weapons to Libya that could not be traced to the United States."

## Syria (Syria's Next)

### Feb–May 2012
*Syria Through a Glass, Darkly*
A lot of people have been asking us whether Libya was our dress rehearsal for Syria.

*U.S. Joins Effort to Equip and Pay Rebels in Syria*
With the help of some Islamic dictatorships, we hope to destabilize Syria enough to get a civil war going there.

*Syria Uprising Creates Fear of Chemical Weapons Spread*

Al-Qaeda is our number 1 mortal enemy everywhere on earth (except for Syria where we are on the same side).

Only Moscow prevents us from setting the Levant on fire.

Help us. Supposing we openly arm Saudi allied religious fanatics and blow up Syria's infrastructure, we'll need a name for the operation.
**@Bro_Pair** Operation Certain Blowback
**@APOVMentarch** "Operation Double-Dip"
**@Len_Day** Operation Lionheart

### June–Aug 2012
Mark our words. With help from Al-Qaeda, Turkey's Islamic president, the Saudis and other absolute monarchs, we're going to free Syria.

*Rebels "Execute" Regime Loyalists in Aleppo*
We've been providing CIA intelligence to anti-Assad fighters. Watch them execute members of a rival clan.

## Sept–Oct 2012

*Fire Sweeps Through Aleppo's 17th-Century Souk*
@ahmadalissa Aleppo's ancient Souk burnt down. National heritage, why?

Less competition for Walmart.

Developing countries have a choice: Either level your bazaars/souks and build strip malls for big box retailers or watch them get bombed.

## Nov–Dec 2012

Further destabilizing Syria could mean security work and eventually reconstruction contracts for our partners. It's too good to pass up.

As for Syria, we believe the ends (a heap of rubble patrolled by our drones), justifies the means (regional war + arming al-Qaeda).

# PART IV

# Enforcing Fear

# 29

## OCCUPY

**Eve of OWS • OWS Begins • Mass Arrests • Occupy Oakland Starts • U Cal Beatings • NYC Eviction • UC Davis Pepper Spraying • Occupy LA Eviction • Tent Monsters, Occupy SF, Occupy DC • Ports Shut Down • Occupy Denver Eviction • NYC Celebrates New Year's • U Cal, Occupy Congress, NZ Eviction • Occupy Oakland Arrests, Occupy DC Eviction**

Unlimited spending on elections by corporations counts as free speech, occupation of a public space by protesters does not. — SecFear

*Occupy Wall Street (OWS or Occupy) began on the third anniversary of the financial crisis on on September 17, 2011. Protests in New York City soon spread across the country and around the world. Tent cities were erected in public squares. Encampments were reminiscent of the occupation of Cairo's Tahrir Square which had precipitated the downfall of Hosni Mubarak seven months before.*

*Always on the lookout for insurrection, the Department began tweeting about the protest movement when it was in the planning stages.*

*The Department took credit for daily brutality and the final dismantling of Occupy sites across the country. While the mainstream media rarely broached the subject, people following the Department on Twitter could see that the crackdowns must*

*have been coordinated. In the months following the Occupations, documents describing interstate surveillance of Occupy by the FBI and a nationally coordinated campaign by Homeland Security to crush the movement would come to light.*

*Department staff reported events across the country by monitoring live video feeds. The livestreamers were the eyes and ears of the world at the occupy sites. Police considered them fair targets for harassment, physical abuse, and arrest. Because of the proximity of the Occupy D.C. sites to DoF headquarters, staff made frequent visits to the encampments. They mingled among the protesters, never giving away their identities.*

*In New York City the press didn't cover OWS in the beginning. The city made it hard for non-mainstream journalists to cover events because few were eligible for press passes, without which the city arrested them. But police made sure even reporters with press passes got attacked.*

## Eve of Occupy Wall Street

If even one banker is inconvenienced by this... — SecFear

@anonops_live 20,000 Protestors To Occupy Wall St.

On Saturday September 17 you can watch us disperse the #OccupyWallStreet protesters.

We're simply going to arrest everyone who's not wearing a suit. It will be as if nothing happened. #OccupyWallStreet #Sept17

@AnonPanama so you can arrest 10,000 people in a day? we'll see about that...

Public Service Message: We're working with your local police to keep politics off the streets.

## Weeks 1–2: OWS Begins and Media Ignores It

For years we have encouraged schools to medicate children who question authority, but it looks like we missed some.
— SecFear

*NYPD Police Pepper Spray Occupy Wall Street Protesters*
First, we corral women into a net, then we mace them. After that, we humiliate them.

**@NYCSep17** any place i stop cops will approach and threaten you.
We trained them well.

We are putting a stop to unregulated activities on Wall Street.

**@OccupyWallSt** Now we're protesting w/ Postal Service workers!
They've gone postal.

☆

US news organizations are not obligated to cover any event we don't ask them to cover. **#takewallstreet #sept17 #occupywallstreet**

Occupy Wall Street doesn't fit the Democrat vs Republican narrative. Why should the mainstream media take the protesters seriously?

## Weeks 3–5: Mass Arrests on Brooklyn Bridge

So as to render the public stupefied, our news media should continue asking over and over: "What is Occupy Wall Street protesting?" — SecFear

Until the demands of OWS protesters fit one of our narratives, our media must continue to insist they have no clear message.

We tricked, trapped and arrested hundreds of protesters on the Brooklyn Bridge this afternoon.

*The Mystery Of The Young Girl Arrested At Brooklyn Bridge*
Our littlest prisoner.

**@martyva** @FearDept: U gotta be kidding me!! Good one NYPD! She's 13 years old.

☆

*JPMorgan Chase Buys Surveillance Equipment for NYPD*
Sweet! A large tax-deductible donation from JPMorgan Chase to the NYPD will profit a maker of surveillance software.

*Financial Giants Put New York City Cops On Their Payroll*
The individual we singled out for arrest at the protest was
distributing fliers critical of Citigroup.

☆

Surveillance pays! After learning a music show host participated in
**#OccupyDC**, NPR fired her.

Americans are free to join OWS protests. They just shouldn't
expect to keep their jobs or ever find work again.

### Weeks 6–7: Occupy Oakland Starts

If OWS was serious about changing our system, they would
have bought some candidates by now. — SecFear

Reinforcements arriving, police line forming. We're monitoring
**#OccupySF** on livestream.

Our police have been firing tear gas canisters at peaceful protesters
in Oakland. **#OccupyOakland**

*Oakland Policeman Throws Flash Grenade Into Crowd Trying To
Aid Badly Injured Person*
Our "Rules of Engagement" for occupied cities are the same as for
Iraq.
**@Angry_Gargoyle** His name is Scott Olsen, an Iraq war vet who served two
tours. Now in a hospital with a fractured skull and swelling of the brain.

*Occupy Oakland: Second Iraq War Veteran Injured After Police
Clashes*
When we don't shoot our veterans in the face, we beat them to a
pulp. **#KayvanSabehgi #ScottOlsen**

We have trained police to behave as if the bottom 99% consists of
two kinds of American: terrorists and potential terrorists.

☆

Potential trouble spots we are monitoring tonight:
**#OccupyOakland**, **#OccupyDC**, **#OWS** and **#OccupySF**.

Poll out today shows alarmingly high level of public support for
OWS.

☆

Hooray! Another journalist (@cecurran) has been fired for appearing at an OWS event. **#FearOWS #WitchHunt**

☆

BREAKING: A mob outside the Goldman Sachs building in NYC is calling for the arrest of President G.W. Bush. **#PrayforBush**

☆

We also attacked **#OccupyRochester** tonight. 16 arrested (including the onlooker who stopped in the park).

☆

We are macing passive **#OccupyTulsa** activists.

☆

*Police Use Bulldozers to Break Up Occupy Richmond*
We used bulldozers to clear away the **#OccupyRichmond** encampment last night.


## Weeks 8–9: University of California Beatings

An occupation anywhere is a threat to our agenda everywhere. — SecFear

The more successful the occupation, the greater our need to dispose of it.

OWS crackdowns are a "teaching moment": U.S. citizens are learning that their exercise of 1st Amendment rights is at our discretion.

UC Berkeley is on our side. They're letting us beat up their students. **#occupycal**

*Police Brutalize Professors and Students at Occupy Cal*
On account of their long hair, female students were the easiest for us to beat up.

☆

The **#OccupyRiverside** People's Kitchen fed students, homeless, working people, poor people, so we tore it down.

**@RepublicanDalek** I ONLY HOPE YOU REMEMBERED TO BURN THE
FOOD SO THAT NOBODY COULD EAT IT OUT OF THE GARBAGE!

☆

*Occupy DC Sets The Record Straight*
Injured **#OccupyDC** protesters think gunning a car at pedestrians
is illegal. We say that depends who the victims are.

☆

We're escalating our intimidation of protesters at
**#OccupyAtlanta**. Have made several arrests.

☆

We join Oakland Mayor Jean Quan in calling for an end to
**#OccupyOakland** and ask campers to leave before we have to
hurt any more people.

To help make the plaza unsafe we had Oakland turn off the lights.

☆

Aussie police appear to be following the example we set for them.

A good measure of our special relationship with Australia is the
force their police use against **#OccupyMelbourne** and
**#OccupySydney**.

☆

Tonight we arrested 24 people in St. Louis.


**Week 9: NYC Eviction – Nov. 15**

> If the technology we deploy against protesters tonight
> proves effective, it will help our corporate partners sell
> more products abroad. — SecFear

*Lobbying Firm's Memo Spells Out Plan to Undermine Occupy
Wall Street*
Who the f--- leaked our lobbying firm's memo?

"Propaganda, as inverted patriotism, draws nourishment from the
sins of the enemy. If there are no sins, invent them." — Ian
Hamilton, 1921

*Cities Struggle to Deal with Occupy Movement*
Important CNN article—based on Dept approved sources—
explains OWS is a source of disease, debt, and violence.

**@NBCNewYork** OWS protesters coming down with the "Zuccotti lung"

Notes conditions resemble Muslim's hajj pilgrimage to Mecca.
Plus STDs, mold.

☆

Staff are monitoring our operations against OWS protesters in
Lower Manhattan on livestream.

We're not allowing press access to areas where we expect to
assault protesters tonight.

**@LindseyChrist** CLASH! Cops with sticks and protesters. Everyone is
screaming. Grand and Centre.

**@paleofuture** New York has achieved full bladerunner.

**@JoshHarkinson** ...I am afraid of walking around because I could get arrested
too.

Josh knows we go after reporters.

**@coreykilgannon** NYT's Colin Moynihan and Robert Stolarik quit Zuccotti to
avoid arrest.

We scared away two NYT reporters.

CNN just went live. Now that the park is mostly cleared out, CNN
knows it's OK to start showing some live pictures.

CNN reporter, allowed on live television now that our crackdown
is mostly over, just said: "there have been no reports of violence."

Thank you to the mainstream media for cooperating with us last
night.

☆

*Violent clashes in Cairo leave two dead and hundreds injured –*
*Nov. 19*
Staff are monitoring a live video feed from Tahrir Square.

**@Arabist** Just heard on State TV: "In the West they suppress protests, so why
can't we?" **#Tahrir**

We lead, the whole world follows.

## Week 9: UC Davis Pepper Spraying

> The Gallery of Memorable Occupy Macings (GMOM)
> brings tears (of joy) to my eyes. GMOM's worth a visit. —
> SecFear

This evening we're conducting land, air and sea operations to prevent **#OccupyDC** from taking Key Bridge. The bridge links DC and Virginia.

☆

*Police Pepper Spraying and Arresting Students at UC Davis*
They sat hunched over, heads tucked in. We sprayed them as if they were insects. **#UCDavis**

**@LadyDeeDoodles** SHAME ON YOU!!

We waterboard the terror suspect, we pepper spray the degenerate.

☆

The occupy sites we won't tell you about: **#OccupyDetroit #OccupyCleveland #OccupyAlbany #OccupyLouisville**

## Week 11: Occupy LA Eviction

> Because the "American Dream" is out of reach for this
> generation, we came up with the idea of giving them the
> "American Nightmare." — SecFear

*Oakland Cops Beat Iraq War Veteran Kayvan Sabehgi*
So far we've seriously injured 2 Iraq veterans. A new video released 11/18 shows what we did to the second.

*Black Friday Mic Check at San Diego Walmart*
We're investigating the infestation of a San Diego WalMart by OWS.

☆

Our idea to use Dodger Stadium to process **#OccupyLA** arrests came from a staff member with CIA experience in Chile.

We have 27 buses and 900 LAPD officers en route to Solidarity Park at this hour.

We're monitoring the situation at **#OccupyLA** on live video.

We have declared an unlawful assembly. We have given the people 8 minutes to go away. We told the cameraman to turn out his light. **#OccupyLA**

We are about to arrest a great-grandmother, religious leaders, veterans, and non-violent observers.  **#OccupyLA**

As soon as we began to make lots of arrests at **#OccupyLA** we ordered the press to leave the area.

☆

BREAKING: We just kicked the press out of **#OccupyPhilly** and read our 3rd & final dispersal order.

We're simultaneously raiding both **#OccupyPhilly** and **#OccupyLA** tonight.

☆

We arrested 292 citizens at **#OccupyLA** last night. One thousand four hundred LAPD took part.

We collect the DNA of arrested **#OccupyLA** protesters to help research treatments for the condition, possible childhood vaccine.

☆

Concerned about hypothetical risks to our own safety, last night we tasered **#OccupyOlympia** protesters.

### Week 12: Tent Monsters, Occupy SF, Occupy DC

If you protest in a way that attracts attention, we're going to arrest you. — SecFear

Staff concerned by reports "Tent Monsters" swarming central business district of Melbourne, Australia.

Occupy Melbourne "Tent Monster" stripped and assaulted by Council workers and police.

☆

An asthmatic protester was having an attack so we took away his inhaler. We wish him well. **#OccupySF**

We arrested 85 protesters at **#OccupySF** during a raid on their camp.

☆

Our prayers are with K-Street lobbyists today. They tell us **#OccupyDC** is making a lot of noise outside their offices.

We just slammed 4 people to the ground and arrested them at **#OccupyDC**.

We deployed 126 vehicles to arrest 46 in the nation's capital today.

☆

The kid was in the park so we hit him in the face. **#OccupyPortland**

## Week 13: Threats to Shut Down Ports

If people want for their communities what we gave away to the corporations, they should talk to the corporations about leasing. — SecFear

We're on high alert. **#OccupyLA**, **#OccupySF**, **#OccupyOakland**, **#OccupyPortland** and **#OccupySeattle** threaten to cut flow of disposable goods from Asia within 4 hours.

Consumer Advisory: West Coast port shutdown planned for Mon Dec. 12 could reduce availability of stuff.

Schedule for Mon: 10:00 Pepper spray; 12:00 Lunch; 13:00 Hit with sticks; 15:00 Gas everyone; 17:00 Break cameras; 20:00 Arrest everyone.

Their plan for today is to shut down all the ports up and down the west coast—along w/ Houston—from Vancouver to San Diego.

☆

We commandeered a homeless outreach van for our Dec. 12 **#OccupyHouston** crackdown.

Staff monitoring livestream report **#TentMonster** sighting in Oakland.

Mounted on horses we charged a line of protesters. On foot we used our batons to hit them.

**@KitOConnell** People who were stepped on by horses considering assault charges. **#d12 #gulfportaction**

**@Ghostpickles** I have never seen tents used to cover people being arrested before today. It was surreal. And dubious. **#d12 #occupyhouston**

We assure you the purpose of the red tent wasn't to gas protesters (only our blue and green tents are built for that).

☆

House Govt Oversight Chair @DarrellIssa wrote the Sec. of the Interior demanding fed. inquiry into health of grass near **#OccupyDC** tents.

## Week 14: Occupy Denver Eviction

Divide the 99%, unite the 1%. — SecFear

They appeared to be sleeping so we roughed them up & made arrests. **#OccupySouthDakota**

☆

Staff have switched to another livestream to monitor our eviction of **#OccupyDenver**.

And we're in full riot gear. We're coming at them, pushing them. We're demanding that everyone exit park. **#OccupyDenver**

**@OccupyDenver** People are saying COPS ARE LIGHTING THINGS ON FIRE. **#OccupyDenver**

This could mean the occupation had a library.

Whenever there's a fire at **#Tahrir**, Egypt state media will say the protesters lit it. Good to hear similar claims about **#OccupyDenver** fires!

**@laurenalesia** I think that, like our successful CIA rendition flights program, the constitution does not apply at high altitude.

Denver, CO altitude is 1609 meters; Bagram Air Base, Afghanistan altitude is 1630 meters.

## Weeks 16–17: NYC Celebrates New Year's

So far we've arrested 50 reporters for the crime of exposing our mistreatment of OWS protesters. — SecFear

**@SabzBrach** Oh God, we're all going to jail.

We lifted a barricade & smashed it into the face of a protester. Now he's bleeding. **#NYPD**

We wanted them to spend New Years Eve in a cage, but protesters are dismantling our steel barricades & tossing them into a big pile. **#NYPD**

We're trying to run over protesters with our scooters.

We just arrested an observer for the National Lawyer's Guild for making a phone call.

Happy New Year. We're arresting everybody.

☆

Moments ago, 60 strong & dressed in riot gear, we swooped thru **#OccupyOakland's** plaza & made indiscriminate arrests.

☆

Staff are monitoring the deteriorating situation at **#OccupyBoston**.

☆

With the barriers down, we're arresting protesters at Zuccotti Park again. **#NYPD**

☆

We arrested three **#OccupyPhilly** protesters today for handing out leaflets.

## Weeks 18–19:  U Cal, Occupy Congress, New Zealand Eviction

We pulled out all the stops in our coordinated coast-to-coast effort to make the Occupy movement look bad. — SecFear

Today we fired rubber bullets at **#occupyuc** students.
**@mmorri** Their tuition has nearly QUADRUPLED over past decade.

☆

A citizen walked into the basement of our Supreme Court wearing an "Occupy" jacket. We arrested him on the spot.

**@castillao** shame on you

☆

To protect Congress from the people, we installed a double ring of fences around Capitol Hill.

**@Casual_Obs** US Capitol is the new "Green Zone." Worked great in Baghdad. **#GreenZone**

**@pbj06** Spring '77, had just finished UW grad school, we drove into DC + onto Capitol Hill at dawn. Only a potbellied security guard.

We used our helicopter to intimidate protesters gathered at the Washington Monument for the **#OccupyCongress** General Assembly.

☆

Over 100 people disrupted a foreclosure auction in Brooklyn & we arrested 26 of them.

☆

25 years ago New Zealand became a Nuclear Free Zone. Today we foiled a Kiwi plot to turn NZ into a Wall Street Free Zone.

Staff are monitoring the situation in New Zealand where the crackdown on **#OccupyAuckland** has begun.

"That's the kind of shit they pull in the States," says a member of **#OccupyAukland** to a police officer.

### Weeks 20–21: Occupy Oakland Arrests, Occupy DC Eviction

Next time you hear an OWS supporter claim life has more to offer than our shadow puppetry, ask how much their show earns. — SecFear

We've encouraged officials to use the phrase "domestic terrorism" to describe the **#OccupyOakland** protest of Jan. 28.

We're snatching people into vans off the streets of downtown Oakland.

Our riot shields are up & we're preparing to charge a sparsely occupied street. **#OccupyOakland**

We've finally located @OakFoSho. He's filming us arresting people from above. **#OccupyOakland**

☆

Today staff used electricity to capture a large human spotted at a campsite. **#OccupyDC**

Having overseen the destruction of Occupy camps from coast-to-coast, it's exciting to think we're about to crush this last base of dissent.

Some of the spectators at **#OccupyDC** could be lobbyists for the 1%. We can't risk gassing or beating them by mistake so its wait & see 4 us.

All police states are not alike. We've tolerated free speech at **#OccupyDC** longer than Egypt's junta held off attacking **#Tahrir** protesters.

Staff member dressed in SWAT gear arrives for crackdown on **#OccupyDC** in a Homeland Security vehicle.

Long, busy day. We made **#OccupyDC** unlivable & beat up people we saw there.

Staff photo shows what we accomplished at **#OccupyDC** today.

Male and female, young and old, we didn't discriminate, we just pushed.

☆

We're about to wipe **#OccupyMiami** off the map. You can follow on livestream.

**#OccupyMiami** protesters are using Bob Marley against us.

☆

BREAKING: We destroyed **#OccupyBuffalo** tonight. We're throwing what's left of their kitchen into a dump truck now.

We arrested 10 **#OccupyBuffalo** protesters.

"Now there's just pollution where there once was something beautiful." — live-streamer BootsOfSolidarity describing what **#OccupyBuffalo** looks like now.

# 30

# SURVEILLANCE

**Facebook • Ending Anonymity • Databases • Privacy Begone! •
Engineering Personal Transparency • Silicon Valley • Cyber
Security • Advice • See Something, Say Something • Telecoms •
New Technology • Sympathy • PSA**

We don't scrap unpopular surveillance projects, we put
them on the back burner and turn up the fear. — SecFear

*The tweets in this chapter, which precede Edward Snowden's leaks
by at least six months, lend perspective on today's so-called
surveillance debate. Apologists for the shadow government claim
"damage" caused by the NSA leaks could irreparably harm the
United States. Reform-minded politicos talk as if passing new laws
limiting NSA activities would restore the Constitution.*

*However, the surveillance system of the U.S. government is
more robust than the totality of spying by NSA. The NSA is but one
of 17 intelligence agencies that comprise the United States
Intelligence Community. According to the Washington Post, there
are 1,271 government organizations and 1,931 private companies
in about 10,000 locations across the United States working on
counterterrorism, homeland security, and intelligence. Forty-nine
percent of the personnel budget for intelligence is outsourced to
private contractors.*

*These tweets remind us that surveillance is the responsibility of
many agencies and corporations. They also point to some*

*remarkable things that were already known about NSA spy programs and highlight the range of efforts being made to eradicate privacy.*

## Facebook

♪ Getting to know you
Getting to know all about you. ♪

Make sure we can find you on Facebook.

Your gut tells you that unless the person had something to hide, they'd be on Facebook.

*Facebook Wants You to Snitch On Friends Not Using Their Real Names*
Facebook is more useful to us when people use real names. Please report any friends that don't.

*House Votes Against Facebook Password Amendment*
Our Congress agrees the 1% can demand the 99% hand over their Facebook passwords as a condition of employment.

## Ending Anonymity

Help us end anonymous speech online. Don't trust anyone Facebook or Google cannot identify for us.

*MA Judge: No Right to Anonymous Speech Online*
You have the right to "anonymous speech on the Internet" unless we take an interest in you.

## Databases

Every day, our collection systems intercept and store 1.7 billion e-mails, phone calls and other types of communications.

*Surveillance State Evils*
We've assembled "on the order of 20 trillion transactions about U.S. citizens with other U.S. citizens."

*Report: Obama's Plan to Harvest and Store US Persons' Data Faced Objections at DHS Privacy Office*
We will be passing whole databases about U.S. civilians to foreign governments for analysis of their own

Relaxes Limits on Use of Data in Terror Analysis
The change announced today marks the revival of "Total Information Awareness"—a database of everything on everybody.

## Privacy Begone!

People don't have human rights online, but some human rights persist offline because our laws are outdated.

WikiLeaks Supporters Lose Court Bid to Protect Twitter Records
We just won the right to obtain everyone's Twitter records!

Feds Snoop on Social-Network Accounts Without Warrants
Did you know we snoop on social media accounts without warrants in real time?

Never having known privacy, we think future generations won't be inclined to ask for it. Especially if all our good little spies get perks.

## Engineering Personal Transparency

Personal Security Weak on Purpose, Fix It
"The cloud is custom-built to spy on users, its lack of security is a prime feature." — cryptome.org

For mere citizens deliberately crippled personal security is no accident, it's Department policy.

## Silicon Valley

The United States Department of Fear is a proud partner of Silicon Valley in the War Against Privacy.

Court Upholds Google-NSA Relationship Secrecy
We're happy that our data partnership arrangements with Google will remain secret.

Our spying guides for Facebook, Verizon, TimeWarner, Gmail, iPhone, etc. are now available online.

CISPA (Cyber Intelligence Sharing and Protection Act) would ensure corporations cannot be held liable for improperly sharing your personal data with us.

It's time to come up with a definition of personal freedom that suits the needs of web companies that profit from data mining.

*Study Shows Continuous Computerized Surveillance Has Negative Effects*
As if we care.

## Telecoms

The United States Department of Fear is a proud partner of the Telecommunications Industry

*American ISPs to Launch Massive Copyright Spying Scheme on July 1*
Better save up. On July 12 our telecom partners begin spying on you. Fines of $150,000 per infringement.

*Police Are Using Phone Tracking as a Routine Tool*
We try to keep cell phone tracking secret "because of possible backlash from the public and legal problems."

## Cyber Security

*JPMorgan's Counter-Terrorism Tool*
To keep the bank's crimes hidden, JP Morgan is deploying counter-terrorism tools to spy on possible whistle-blowers.

There's a wealth of online security measures available to Department staff. As for ordinary citizens like yourself, well good luck.

## Surveillance Advice

Maintaining consistency in your daily routine makes our job a lot easier.

Never try to observe us the way we observe you.

Whenever you step away from your computer, even for a short time, be sure to carry your mobile tracking device. Thank you.

To the extent you interact with persons under surveillance you're opening yourself to become a target of surveillance.

**@sysprog3** "customers ... antsy about frequenting a store or restaurant that's been under NYPD surveillance"

If you imagine there's a vision behind the surveillance society we're building, we'll have you labeled a conspiracy theorist.

### See Something, Say Something

> ♪ Come on people now
> Spy on your brother
> Everybody get together
> Try to fear one another
> Right now ♪

**@saniasufi** i don't know whether to laugh or cry.

**@MommaKnows_Best** and there we have the real definition of #SeeSomethingSaySomething

*Improving the Public's Awareness and Reporting of Suspicious Activity*
Our study looks at ways to get citizens to file more Suspicious Activity Reports on their neighbors.

*"If You See Something, Say Something" Sports League and Team Partnerships*
We've enlisted major sports teams to encourage you to spy on each other.

*T Riders Can Report Suspicious Activity With New Phone App*
**@jaykelly26** Oh look a new @FearDept app for your phone.

**@jaykelly26** @tentmonster thats exactly what Im gonna use it for... reporting @FearDept to @FearDept

*Angry Birds, Meet Jailbirds: New App Helps You Snitch on Your Friends*
Spying on your neighbor for us? Now you can send us reports in real time.

See Something, Say Something, Leave Before the Drone Arrives.
**#futurecampaignslogans**

## New Surveillance Technology

*"Black Box" in Your Car Raising Questions*
New resources like your smartphone and the black box in your car make our job easier.

For your safety ;) all new cars sold after 2015 must contain a "black box."

*Drive-by Scanning: Officials Expand Use and Dose of Radiation for Security Screening*
Our unmarked X-ray vans can look inside vehicles for drugs, explosives or protesters.

*Apple Patents Mobile Camera That Other People Can Shut Off*
Apple patents mobile camera that we can shut off.

*Yellow Dots of Mystery: Is Your Printer Spying on You?*
Not only your PC works for us. Other office machines do too.

*Big Brother Just Got Scarier: Japanese CCTV Camera Can Scan 36 Million Faces per Second*
We will soon be able to recognize ANYONE instantly.

*Greg of San Jose, CA Finds 2 New GPS Tracking Devices Hidden on His SUV*
We want them back.

## Sympathy

How are you vulnerable? What's your breaking point? We're working with our corporate partners to get to know you better.

Knowing we're reading your emails, monitoring your phone calls, searches, transactions, even tracking your whereabouts…

It must suck knowing you're being spied upon…
**@anon_byter** Not knowing would suck more.

## PSA (Public Service Announcement)

Stop leaving rude messages in your email accounts for us to read.

Reminder: Always tag photos of friends with their names and location (we can get the date from the EXIF data)

# 31

## DOMESTIC DRONES

**Opportunities • About Our Drone Program • Perspective • Models • Drone Associates • Law • Police • Marketing Drones • Drone Propaganda • Harassing Opponents • Negating Risks • Silent Spring • Future of Drones**

Don't shoot the drones. — SecFear

*With the war in Afghanistan winding down, the drone manufacturing industry saw an opportunity to sell drones to law enforcement agencies. Observing the way drones were being used overseas, citizens expressed concern when plans to fly them over the Homeland were announced.*

### Opportunities

Certainly drones have proven a cost-effective means of terrorizing foreign populations. Can drones do the same for the Homeland or will they all get shot down?

*Congressional Report Warns Drones Could Track Faces, Never Leave Sky*

Deadly drone strikes make our politicians look tough, generate huge profits for the UAV industry, and pacify our scaredy-cat citizens.

*Talk of Drones Patrolling US Skies Spawns Anxiety*
So far, so good.

Once our advanced drone technology gets in the hands of terrorists, we're going to have to seriously rethink civil liberties.

## About Our Drone Program

*Drone Group Doubled Lobbying Expenses Last Year*
Year after drone lobby group @AUVSI doubled its lobbying budget, we agreed to open U.S. skies to drones.

*Despite Problems, a Push to Expand Domestic Use of Drone*
Sixty-seven lawmakers have received nearly $8 million in campaign contributions from drone-related PACs.

*Ten Years Since First Deadly Drone Strike, Industry Gathers in London*
DoD drone budget 2010–2015 includes $24 billion for new drones and upgrades. CIA drone budget is not available. Sorry.

*Is a Military Drone Base Coming to Your Hometown?*
We've identified 110 potential bases for drone operations at military installations in 39 states.

Curious how long our drones will be allowed to hover outside your window? Drone rules are coming out next week.

## Drones in Perspective

Either we get to kill foreigners with our drones or we'll make your kids do it.

Drones evoke "original fear." Humans haven't feared flying predators since pterodactyls terrorized our ancestors…

Civilization has always meant human beings could live without fear of being killed by non-human predators. We changed that.

If only we had drones back in the 1800s we could have put the Indians in shantytowns without having to fight so many wars against them.

@cossa68 So I just told my coworkers there will soon be surveillance drones over our city and no one seemed to mind. What planet am I on?

Ours.

## Models

We have a drone "the size of a pizza capable of hovering outside your window for several hours."

**@DemocritusJr** Alas, this just makes most Americans hungry

**@Tom_Godell** Regular or thin crust? And no anchovies please.

*Insect-Sized Spy Drone Robots Unveiled*
Our Insect Spy Drone has a camera, mic & needle for DNA sample. It injects micro RFID tracking device.

*Air Force Deploys Newest Armed Stealth Drone to Afghanistan*
Stealth Avenger Drone (aka Predator C) is the successor to Predator and Reaper. It will deliver 2,000 lb missiles.

*US Draws Up Plans for Nuclear Drones*

## Drone Associates

*Demand for Unmanned Aircraft "Insatiable"*
Tom Faller, Chief of Drones at Homeland Security & a leader of the biggest drone industry group calls demand for drones "insatiable."

*Director of Federal Drone Program Targeted in Ethics Inquiry*
Oops.

*General: "Use Drones to Kill" the Taliban in Pakistan*
Ret. Gen. Keane, now a director at General Dynamics (maker of Predator B), urges us to expand use of drones in Pakistan.

## Law

*Drones, Dogs and the Future of Privacy*
Curious why it's legal for our spy drone to hover outside your window? To the courts, that's a "flying police dog."

## Police

*Police Apologize for Not Keeping Council in Loop on New Drones*
We've been handing money out to police departments so they can have secret drone programs.

*NYPD Reportedly Experimenting with Drones To Monitor NYC*
Don't look so shocked, you knew this was coming.

## Marketing Drones

*Demand Rises for Civilian Drones*
The world's hungriest market for drones? Our 19,000 law enforcement agency offices.

*Drone Market to Total $89 Billion Over Next Ten Years*
Yes!

## Drone Propaganda

*1 in 3 U.S. Warplanes is a Robot*
Most appropriately, a Congressional report highlights benefits of drones while ignoring their unique vulnerabilities.

Disseminate propaganda toward winning public support for vastly increased use of drones for domestic law enforcement.
**#NewYearsResolution**

*Drones to Scour the Clouds for Hurricanes' Secrets*

*UAVs May Play Big Role in Developing Arctic*

*Drones: Not Just for Military Use*

*Civilian Drones That Can Dust Crops, Find Lost Toddlers & Wash Skyscraper Windows Are Just Years Away*

*New Drone To Help Joggers Keep a Steady Pace*

*Drone Development in Northwest Poses No Privacy Threats*

*UAVs May Play Big Role in Developing Arctic*

*Unmanned Air Vehicles (UAVs) Have Considerable Application in Oil Exploration*

## Harassing Opponents of Drones

*Anti-Drone NYC Street Artist Arrested*
We finally arrested that anti-drone NYC street artist.
**@StanleyCohenLaw** Whew, I feel much better now! Keep up the good repression, i mean work!

Can we smear opponents of drones as un-American, reckless, or crazy? At first we should try everything and then see what sticks.

## Negating Risks

*Pilots: Drones Pose Major Safety Threat in Civilian Air Space*

*Drone Lobby Cracks Open American Skies*
We decided it's OK for drones to fly in civil airspace. Pilots worry drones can't see them; can't take evasive action.

*Border Patrol Using Drones to Battle Marijuana Trade*
We'll lose a few airliners to collisions with stray drones, but that's a small price to pay for finding the marijuana.

@**Kaveros** When the drones start colliding with passenger jets here, you should just blame it on terrorists hacking the drones.

If thousands of drones are to surveil the Homeland cost-effectively, Congress may have to wave liability for drone manufacturers.

*Drones Can Be Hijacked via GPS Spoofing Attack*
Don't hack the drones.

## Silent Spring

You won't know whether you're shooting at a bird or one of our drones.

*Pentagon Reveals Tiny $4m Nano Hummingbird Flying Spy*
We anticipate humans will shoot every bird out of the sky as a precaution against our new bird drones.

When all the birds are gone we'll act surprised. We'll say "who could have imagined this consequence of making drones look like birds."

## Future of Drones

*Many Fear Domestic Drone's Potential for Lethal Force*
Having given up hope of banning domestic drone surveillance, civil society groups just beg us not to arm them.

@**Kaveros** How does that work? Are the drones going to swoop at crowds of protesters and strafe them indiscriminately with rubber bullets?

*DoD Developing Super Precise Drone*
Too bad the kill list itself is based on shit intel.

U.S. citizens live in fear. For safety's sake, we think many will pay to have surveillance drones follow them around.

**@Kbkibbe** How much will they pay to have our drones follow them? A nice cooling fan over my head would be nice in the summer.

When our skies are full of drones, it won't be "pleasant" to go outdoors. Silver lining is this will increase the appeal of shopping malls.

**@annakissed36** Where do you live that has shopping malls that don't have hundreds of "security" cameras?

**@MissShevaughn** California is so progressive... their shopping malls don't have roofs...

Our vision for the Counter-Terrorism Channel (CTC) is 24/7 live drone footage from across the Middle East.

Give drones a chance.

# 32

## SILENCING WHISTLE-BLOWERS

The Threat • WikiLeaks • Assange • Manning • Anonymous • Apple

We charged Bradley Manning with the same crime as seven other whistle-blowers: Informing the public. — SecFear

*The Espionage Act of 1917 provided the Obama administration with the means to prosecute seven citizens. This was more than the total number charged under all previous administrations. The administration also stepped up harassment of social activists.*

*In going after activists and whistle-blowers, the U.S. government has recruited the support of industry. For example, no sooner had WikiLeaks released the State Department cables than Visa, MasterCard and PayPal agreed not to process legal donations to the new media organization, effectively starving WikiLeaks of funds for its legal defense and growth.*

### The Threat of Whistle-blowing

*State Dept Moves to Fire Author of Book Critical of Iraq Reconstruction Effort*
We're firing Van Buren, author of "We Meant Well." Book exposes our fake & costly Iraq reconstruction projects.

*A View From Inside the NSA's Warrantless Surveillance Program*
Although the threat abated, surveillance of Americans continued. This troubled some of our longtime NSA employees.

*The Rise and Fall of Jeremy Hammond: Enemy of the State*
Expose our corporate partners' complicity in our crimes and we'll
come after you with everything we've got.

## WikiLeaks

*Banking Blockade*
Our partnership with big banks against WikiLeaks has cost the
group $50 Million in lost donations.

**@stevilism** I want to donate to WikiLeaks & support Assange but I'm afraid if I
do I will be on some FBI or CIA hit list. I'm not kidding

"WikiLeaks has blood on hands in digital 9/11" — Senator
Lieberman

"There's enormous potential damage for the United States ... in
these leaks." — Wolf Blitzer

*Poll: Americans Concerned WikiLeaks Dump Will Hurt the U.S.*
Proof our side is winning.

**@miamibeach** I just followed @WikiLeaks Should I be scared?
Yes.

*After Cablegate, Enforced Ignorance*
State Dept. employees forbidden to look at WikiLeaks cables.

Warning from Amb. Kurtzer: "The fact that [a WikiLeaks cable] is
in the public domain does not make it available for public
viewing."

"Frmr State Dept official warned "public may be breaking the law
by looking at or talking about [WikiLeaks cables]."

**@TRON_SMSP** The US Fear Dept is scaring students and professors out of
reading WikiLeaks docs.

## Julian Assange

*U.S. Calls Assange "Enemy of State"*
We have declared Julian Assange an Enemy of the State. Fear him.

*Assange Says He Fears for His Life If Extradited to U.S.*
Assange, seeking asylum in the Ecuador embassy in London, says
he fears we'll kill him.

*Saudis Second Largest Swedish Arms Buyers*
If Sweden has second thoughts about handing Assange over to us
for his espionage trial, we'll threaten to stop buying their weapons.

## Chelsea (Bradley) Manning

Manning's leaks spread freedom, opening-up societies around the
world. Where did he get the idea those things might be part of his
job?

@**Edpilkington** BRADLEY MANNING "I was authorised to have 20 minutes
sunshine call" – ie 20 mins outside his cell - in chains - every 24 hours

It's not torture if we let you out of your cell for 20 minutes a day.

*Bradley Manning Trial: US Government Ordered to Release
WikiLeaks Damage Assessments*
When speaking anonymously, what we say contradicts our official
position that WikiLeaks caused "substantial" damage.

There are "look forward" & "look backwards" crimes. Ordering
torture is the 1st, embarrassing those who order torture is the 2nd.

## Anonymous

*The Stuxnet Story and Some Interesting Questions*
Remember our fearmongering about Anonymous attacking
infrastructure? We attacked those systems first.

@**USAnonymous** The @FearDept would have you believe that the Anonymous
agenda is anything other than humanitarian. Like terroristic.

@**xACE_9x** @YourAnonNews you should be proud @FearDept and it's
affiliates seem to fear hackers. So they write special laws just for you.

*Exclusive: FBI Escalates War On Anonymous*

*Insider Tells Why Anonymous "Might Well Be the Most Powerful
Organization on Earth"*

What's our Achilles heel?

## Apple

When faced with "divisive issues" corporations tend to side with
the Department. We're often their biggest customers.

*Apple Removes WikiLeaks from App Store*
Although they rejected a WikiLeaks App, Apple approved
"WikiLeaks Defender" (you're a TSA agent fighting WikiLeaks).

*Apple Rejects App that Tallies Deaths from US Drone Strikes*
*THREE Times Claiming It's "Objectionable and Crude."*
Apple rejected "drones+ App yet approved "UAV Fighter Free"
produced by TransLumen, a military defense contractor.

Apple knows we don't want informed citizens.

*As It Lobbies For Tax Holiday, Apple Admits Hoarding Cash*
*Overseas To Avoid Paying Taxes*
Why won't Apple approve that Drones App and piss us off?
Consider the taxes they owe us but don't want to have to pay.

*Google Maps: Thanks for the App, Here's My Personal Data*
If you're installing Google Maps on your iPhone, make sure your
home address is up to date. Thanks.

We're the eye in iPhone.

**@AlcibiadesSlim** Should we eat of The Apple to better know Fear?

# 33

# NOWHERE TO HIDE

**Australia • Austria • Canada • Sweden • UK • Other
Exemplars**

Imagine what a world it would be if all the other countries
remade themselves in our image. — SecFear

*Close allies are copying the Department's programs, sometimes
surpassing the United States in the execution of them, even coming
up with new approaches for spreading fear. Freedom-loving
people who don't approve of the American system are discovering
there is nowhere to hide.*

## Australia

### *Australia – Surveillance*

*Coming Soon: Facial Recognition Instead of Passport for Travel
from Australia to New Zealand*
Wow!

*Full-body Scans Rolled Out at All Australian International
Airports After Trial*
Congratuations L3G! Australia will force every visitor to submit to
an L-3 body scan.

*U.S. Airport Full Body Scanners Too Unreliable to Use, Germany Says*
The Germans realized the airport body scan machines we sell to countries like Australia don't work.

*ASIO (Australia Security Intelligence Organisation) Eyes Green Groups*
@**Beigemonster** Good to see that conservation groups are being rebranded as Terrorists by government.

### *Australia – Preference for Assassinations*

*The Battle for Syria*
In this video (from 8'45") your foreign minister spoke casually about doing "an assassination." If only other foreign ministers would talk like that. **#respect**

@**hersairness** what, pray, is your suggestion for Syria where a dictator will see over 33,000 of his own civilians killed without compromising?

More people died in Iraq after we put Saddam out of business than before, but our good intentions are all that matters.

@**NOH8ER** But, but, you don't *have* good intentions. Your intentions are selfish.

Shh! Please. @hersairness probably doesn't believe that about the Department or our FM for Australia. No need to bring that up.

### Austria

*Two WikiLeaks-Sympathisers Were Charged for Walking too Slowly in Front of the U.S. Embassy*
Bravo Austria! You'd think these people wrote the book on Homeland security.

@**timeoutcorner**: Actually Austria did write the book! Klemens von Metternich invented the police state.

### Canada

### *Canada - Cooperation*

*Harper Government Omnibus Crime Bill: Canadian Justice Gets a Major Makeover*
More like us: Canada to increase surveillance, build prisons, have mandatory minimum sentences.

*Prison Privatization: Canada Mulls Contracting Services to Companies Lobbying for Correctional Work*
Congratulations Geo Group Inc. for lobbying Canada to privatize its prisons. **#MoreLikeUs**

*Terrorism Monitor Closely Watched Occupy Protests*
Canada's Integrated Terrorism Assessment Centre (ITAC) monitors Occupy protests for us.

*"Baby Steps" to US Agents on Canadian Soil: RCMP*
Canada has invited Fear Dept. staff (FBI, DEA) to begin working on Canadian soil.

If Canadians don't make our staff feel welcome, we'll treat them like Americans.

*Alberta Set to Become Hub for Drone Innovation*
Oil-rich Alberta is set to become a hub for drone innovation. We'll be testing UAV technology on the local population.

*Ottawa Launches Alberta Counterterrorism Unit*
Canada is setting up a new counter-terrorism bureaucracy to defend the property of our oil companies.

*U.S. Can Share Canadian Border Info Under Privacy Deal*
U.S. will be allowed to share Canadian border info under new privacy charter.

### *Canada – Environment*

*Harper Government's Muzzling of Scientists a Mark of Shame for Canada*
Where loyalty's a condition of employment for journos, civil servants, scientists.

*Critics Pan Instructions to Environment Canada Scientists at Montreal Conference*
**@NFSSmith** Fear Dept of Canada. Harper Gov't is now ACTIVELY preventing scientists from direct media access!

**@helenspitzer** My dad and my uncle had more freedom as scientists in communist Czechoslovakia. That is not hyperbole. I'm incensed.

*Canadian Government Overhauling Environmental Rules to Aid Oil Extraction*
Our corporate partners kindly asked Canada to rewrite all its environmental laws & Canada said OK.

*Canadian Military Demands Removal of Counterinsurgency Manual from Public Intelligence*
Good to see Canada's military harassing a group of researchers who posted a WikiLeaks document.

### Canada – Foreign Policy

*Canadian Defence Minister Defends Use of Military Drones*
Canada's minister of defense applauds our drone killing spree.

*DND Removes Report on Killing of Canadian Soldier by Israeli Forces*
Canada knows that when Israel murders Canadians, cover-up is a shared responsibility.

### Canada – Surveillance

*Canada Will Spy on People, Politely*
Canada has graciously wired a major airport with microphones so we can eavesdrop on their terrorists' conversations.

*Electronic Snooping Bill a "Data Grab": Privacy Advocates*
Oh quit whining Canada, we already have your boring data.

*Opposition to Canada's Impending Surveillance Legislation Grows*
Canada "will allow [police] to force identification of anonymous online Internet users."

*"Let's Not Talk About Statistics... Let's Talk About Danger." — Vic Toews*
The **#TellVicEverything** campaign in support of online criminality is the biggest social media backlash Governor Harper has ever faced.

Tonight supporters of online criminality are attacking Governor Harper, a true friend of the Department. **#Pray4GovHarper**

### Canada – Human Rights

*Canada Copying "Elements of the USA PATRIOT Act that Were Found Unconstitutional."*
They're stealing the best parts!

*Fury as Quebec Passes Law to Stifle Student Fee Protests*
Kudos to Quebec for taking away the right to demonstrate and shutting universities.

*Anti–Protest Law Lands Canada on UN Human Rights Watch List*
Our partner.

**@der_bluthund** Canada is a new & disturbing situation, so the UN is right to flag it on the Human Rights Watch List.

We know a country's been a good ally of ours when they get put on the Human Rights Watch list.

**@WCM_JustSocial**: "client" not "ally"

*Canada Lawmakers Ban Masks at Protests*
Best thing about our Canadian parliament banning masks at protests is the 10 year prison term.

*What's Wrong with Canada's Federal Whistleblower Legislation*
Our friends in Ottawa dub their new whistleblower gag law the "Accountability Act."

**@canuckleslie** hey have you guys been coaching our gov't?

### Sweden

*Sweden Violated Torture Ban in CIA Rendition*
We love Sweden.

*IKEA Is as Bad as Wal-Mart*
Another thing we love about Sweden.

*Further Devious Reports on Julian Assange in the Swedish National Television*
We endorse the Swedish state TV campaign against Assange.

### Sweden – Human Rights

*Sweden: Arms Exports Reach Record Level*
Last year Sweden sold the most weapons in the world, per person.

Sweden's arms sales have increased by 350% in just 10 years. Twice as many countries buy its weapons today as twenty years ago. **#respect**

*Nobel Peace Prize Jury Under Investigation*
Given that Sweden exports the most weapons per capita, why would the PeacePrize be anti-military?

@**allafloxninja** Stockholm County Administrative Board oversees the Nobel Foundation & manages prize assets. Follow the money.

Everyone agrees the original Nobel Peace Prize criteria ("best work for the abolition or reduction of standing armies") is bad for business.

## United Kingdom

We have a British oil company washing away the oil in the Gulf and a British bank laundering Mexico's drug money.

Our extradition treaty with the UK gives us unchecked powers over British subjects whose alleged crimes were not committed on American soil.

*Google Reveals "Terrorism Video" Removals*
At UK police request, Google removed 640 YouTube videos the bobbies say promote terrorism.

*Ex-FBI Informant: Muslim Spying is "All About Entrapment"*
Instead of telling Google to remove videos that promote terrorism, we have our FBI informants convince Muslim–American kids to watch them.

### *UK – Foreign Policy*

@**tenpercent** new man in charge of buying all the UK's weapons is... BAE systems' pet MP... Gerald Howarth!
Music to our ears!

*Foreign Travel Advice Ecuador*
So many Ecuadorians support Julian Assange that the UK has issued a "Travel Warning" for the country.

### UK – Surveillance

*British PM Proposes Social Media Ban*
Not to worry, this twitter account won't be affected.

*BBC, ITN and Sky News Give Riot Footage to Police*
UK government continues to inspire us.

*Woman Jailed After al-Qaida Terrorist Material Found on Her Phone*
UK woman who had ~~CIA's~~ al-Qaida's "Inspire Magazine" in her mobile phone was jailed for a year on Thursday.

### UK – Policing

*Prevent: A Totally Illiberal Strategy*
Prevent, new UK counter-terrorism strategy, affirms insight of George W. Bush that they hate us for our freedoms.

*Private Contractors to Build and Run Police Station in Britain*
@neil21 Way ahead of you @FearDept

*Three Arrested at Heathrow on Suspicions of Terrorism*
When we saw what they were reading we knew they must be terrorists.

*UK Green Lights Use of Military Style Drones Over the Skies of Britain.*
HUGE drone market (they love surveillance).

### Other Exemplars

*Honduras to Build Three Privately-Run "Model Cities"*
Honduras, the hub for our Central American operations, is creating democracy-free "model cities" where the constitution won't apply.

*Kite-Flyers to be Booked Under Terrorism Act*
Good move, Pakistan.

# 34

# COMMUNITY OUTREACH

## Community Outreach • Overheard • Feedback • Questions • Replies • Requests

Just about everybody out there believes at least some of our bullshit. — SecFear

*One of the goals of the Department's social media initiative has been to humanize the enterprise. The Department has made an effort to connect with individuals struggling to become more fearful. Sometimes that means taking questions, listening and advising just like an older sibling.*

## Community Outreach

**@whoopingcough** As an American, I spy on myself to conserve our limited tax revenue.

What are you doing for us?

♪ Come on people now / Spy on your brother / Everybody get together / Try to fear one another / Right now ♪

**@analoguepilot** @FearDept please dont sing. you'll just drone on and on.

We don't preach to the choir. Rather, we coach the folks sitting in the back pews to sing on key. Do you follow?

Are you a political scientist with an idea for a new war? Are you an engineer with a design for a new weapon? We'd love to hear from you!

Are you an economist with an idea for a new austerity measure? Are you a novelist with a new terror plot? We'd love to hear from you!

**@skeez** What is America going to be scared of next?

Everyday we ask ourselves this question.

Evil Empire (1982), New World Order (1992), Axis of Evil (2003), _____ (2014).

**@mikebardenkRaap** ya ever hear this1? the only thing we have to fear is fear itself?

FDR said that. World wasn't so dangerous back then.

If you talk about the conspiracy we'll label you a conspiracy monger.

More pervasive wiretapping? Fewer trials? More defense spending? More drone strikes? Bomb bomb bomb Iran? What would make you feel safer?

Time to bring back enhanced interrogation? Longer prison terms for drug crimes? We're looking for profitable ways to make you feel safer.

## Overheard

**@BrknSdwlkFrm** Makes it hard as fuck for @FearDept to come in guns blazing when every police officer has a key & I'm rolling CCTV everywhere.

**@mindofH** democracy is a system of government wherein:
(a) you're free to speak, until you
(b) make sense and
(c) @FearDept labels you a terrorist.

**@strikelawyer** @mikedelic Make sure you run your thoughts by @FearDept You wouldn't want to wind up on a list.

**@mikedelic** @strikelawyer lol. I am still in my 30s but because of @feardept all of my hair has turned white!

**@fullmetalmarty** I hope some people are smarter than the @FearDept and @SecFear think we all are.

**@jaykelly26** Nobody knows where I am right now, except for @FearDept.

**@awesomechairs** I mean I'd move to the States but what with all the wiretapping and Comcast and everything.

Not our type so no loss.

**@TranceWolf** Are Americans that stupid or is the Fear Dept that good?

## Feedback

**@firehorse1200** Fear & anxiety now pervades our home. Our cook & kid's nanny are panic-stricken. Thanks. You make augmenting their paranoia easy.

**@CobaltKitsune** I hate you. I hate you so much for forcing me to put my dreams on hold so I can fix your problems

**@d3fN** I am no longer a person, I am a list of GPS locations and communications. **#freedom**

**@DavidKisHere** I trust you like I trust the worth of Federal Reserve Notes.

**@Aqibnoor** some people from your country trashes my country all the time, and call it something like hell for all the women of the world.

**@indiscreetmuse** We are living a SiFi nightmare. Well, sans the fiction.

**@JPDelancey** thinking u should start national fear day, where everyone is too scared to go out b/c terrorists

**@JSDwyer** Dear @FearDept, George Orwell's "1984" was not meant as an instruction manual. Sincerely yours, Occupy.

**@kade_ellis** hey @feardept did you know that someone (@DHSgov) is impersonating you on Twitter? That's fucked up.

**@LordDunalley** Next time you chainsaw through a door and hold woman and toddler at gunpoint, get the right house.

**@miamiaman** Fear is the cheapest room in the house. I would like to see you living in better conditions ~ Hafiz of Persia

**@mindofH** reason is treason, under new @FearDept guidelines.

**@OccupyWallStNYC** If you're trying to scare us off twitter, @FearDept, keep trying, because we have nothing to hide.

**@SysReboot** sorry, i live by a moral & ethical code. that's a bit beyond corporate laws lol

**@tentmonster** can we get an app to report government thugs location ?

**@thereal_Yoda** Fear is the path to the dark side. Fear leads to anger. Anger leads to hate. Hate leads to suffering.

**@TheRealKeori** Your work on constant replay in amtrak stations is very well done. Love co-option of "grassroots" to describe campaign of fear.

**@thestatesucks** the populace is catching on.

@**AbuSnu** you've got some real assholes in charge

@**KremlinHotline** in Soviet Russia, government have ways of making you talk. In America, government have ways of keeping you quiet. #**Manning**

## Questions

@**DFENS79** I've finished building my bunker. Now what?

@**SassyTeesa** What in the world is a do not kill list???? #**thisworldisgettingtooweirdforme**

@**2JZJay** Im just waiting on you guys to offer me a job or do I need to learn Farsi first?

@**maggiex17xbiebs** I wanna do Habitat for Humanity but my mom is scared of terrorists in those countries.

Mother knows best.

@**_wmg** when is Free Speech Hour today?

Ended at 4:30.

@**BiOzZ** how much money should i shell out of my pocket to make me feel safe again?

@**changa** what is the minimum yearly donation I would need to make to you to guarantee I will not be assassinated?

@**cheesyenergy55** what country are you guys planning on bankrupting next?

@**GarnetLynne** is that a knock at my front door?

@**PGEddington** @GarnetLynne They won't knock.

@**jwindz** Why do I live in such a paranoid country?

@**miamiaman** & anyway u know where the people who disagree live right?

@**MindDetonat0r** What legitimacy does @FearDept have when support for Israel and the Saudi police-state endangers Americans

Don't ever question our legitimacy.

@**NolanLiberty** Who should I be afraid of this week?

@**pena88q** Just wondering why Bob Marley denied shooting the deputy but thought admitting he shot the sheriff would be a-okay.

@**samknight1** you weren't behind the Chris Hayes smear campaign by any chance, were you?

@**sl3ight** Is @FearDept a sponsor of the face eating zombie apocalypse?

**@steveaperry1976** I am scared of the threat, 2660 miles away in Iran, should I give more money to the military contractors?

**@whoopingcough** We're the Little broken-down, 2nd class, beat around the head and neck, fuck'n Engine That Could, right?

**@Wind2Energy** When will the big banks start to hunt us down with Creditor Drones?

**@JohnCornyn** I would love a clear statement of our national security interests and a plan for victory

Sorry, that's classified.

*Man Killed in Freak Accident with Swan*
**@024601** Swans have killed more Americans this year than terrorism has. Swans. We gonna have a war on them next?

**@ACLU_Mass** What's terrorism again?

**@ahmadalissa** how can USA talk about changing other regimes with 50 million Americans under poverty line and 3 million Americans incarcerated?

**@mindthetiller** I'm a college student looking to earn some beer money. Can I get cash for spying on my school's Muslim students?

**Replies**

Americans need to feel the Department is responsive to their fears.

@Vixen_Anonymous President Obama is not authorized to tweet from this account.

@_sugarfix Yes, getting people to believe in really stupid conspiracy theories is part of our operation.

@allshiny Yes, the Department is well aware of what we're putting you through.

@awesomechairs Flattering us won't get you a green card.

@clearcup We're still in D.C. For security reasons having to do with accessing a public website, the location may flip around.

@gumbosplat We're not the Name-Your-Own-Fear-Department.

@mdupray @tedleew Why do you nickel & dime our OccupyDC operation? You want them to look at our other policing, bombing and drug warring costs?

## Requests

**@AlcibiadesSlim** ff @FearDept please keep me off the Kill List.

# *AFTERWARD*

You'll tell your grandkids you helped us destroy America in order to save it. Yes, you will. And we'll be listening for any hint of sarcasm. — SecFear

Stop us if you can.
**@AnonyOps** Challenge accepted

**@_cypherpunks_** If you want to conquer the @FearDept, don't sit home and think about it. Go out and get busy. (Inspired by Dale Carnegie)

The world is a terrifying place. Good night from Washington.
**@Kallisti** I hope the bed bugs bite, you fuckers!

# CONTACT

Some of you may find it reassuring to know that to date not a single follower of the Department has been assassinated.
— SecFear

You can follow Fear Department (@FearDept) on Twitter. The web address is http://twitter.com/FearDept. The Department also maintains a public blog at FearDepartment.com.

If you have concerns, the email address for the Office of the Secretary of Fear is Stag3@FearDepartment.com.

If this book has left you feeling more fearful, please leave a review on Amazon.